# In Search of

# TIMOTHY

# WORKBOOK

# In Search of
# TIMOTHY
## WORKBOOK

Tony Cooke

# Contents

# In Search of
# TIMOTHY
## WORKBOOK

# Introduction

*"These things I write to you . . . so that you may know*
*how you ought to conduct yourself in the house of God,*
*which is the church of the living God,*
*the pillar and ground of the truth."*

–1 Timothy 3:14–15

You are at the beginning of an incredible journey that can transform your life and impact your destiny! The *In Search of Timothy* series not only explores the roles of Timothy and other biblical figures who served the plan of God by serving others, it also is specifically targeted to helping *you* become the servant, worker, and leader that God intends you to be in the Body of Christ.

This workbook corresponds directly to the *In Search of Timothy* textbook and the CD and DVD series. You can work through this material individually, but we feel you will receive the most benefit by working through the material as a member of a group. Discussion and interaction with others can add to what you receive from these lessons.

Each chapter in this workbook contains the following:

## Packing for the Trip

🚗 This section tells you which video to watch (or which CD to listen to) and which pages of the textbook to read. The reading assignment will correspond to what is taught on the video.

# The Expressway

The Expressway is a concise summary of what is taught in each lesson. It's a snapshot or the main points of what you'll want to know.

## Historical Markers

These are selected quotes by others that will reinforce and bring further illumination to the teaching. As you work through the principles that are taught in this material, it's good to know that wise people, both modern and throughout history, have articulated many of the same ideas.

### Historical Marker

*"Whatever you are, be a good one."*

–Abraham Lincoln

## Fuel Stop

These are scriptures that support the teaching. Because the Bible is our guide in matters of faith and practice, it is important to have a solid foundation in the Word of God as we explore the significance of the local church, the importance of teamwork, and our specific assignments in the Body of Christ.

### FUEL STOP

**Galatians 6:9–10**

9 And let us not grow weary while doing good, for in due season we shall reap if we do not lose heart.

10 Therefore, as we have opportunity, let us do good to all, especially to those who are of the household of faith.

## The Scenic Route

The Scenic Route includes summaries and excerpts from the main body of the teaching. There will be some fill in the blanks as you go through this section. Don't get hung up on getting the exact right word. What is most important is that you get the concept, the gist, or the idea. If you need a little help, we have put all the answers at the back of the book in the Answer Key.

 ## Inspection Station

This section is made up of multiple choice questions. The answers to these questions are also in the back of the book in the Answer Key.

 ## Unpacking the Principles

Toward the end of each chapter are some questions for personal reflection and/or discussion. This gives individuals an opportunity to consider how they can apply the principles that are being taught.

 ## Off Road

This is a brief teaching that is not covered in the textbook or in the videos. It's bonus material that will enhance and reinforce the principles being taught.

## Travelogue

## Travelogue

This is simply a blank page where you can write out your personal reflections about what you're learning.

## Thoughts for Group Leaders

As a group facilitator, you have the opportunity to make this learning experience more meaningful for those going through the *In Search of Timothy* experience. Here are some thoughts to help you be a more effective leader throughout this series:

- We suggest opening (and perhaps closing) the sessions with prayer. It's important for people going through this material to have their hearts open to hear what God is saying to them and to be open to growing into all that God wants them to become.

- Know the material yourself. Make sure that you've done the reading assignment from the textbook and have watched the video ahead of time. By working through the lesson in the workbook ahead of time, you'll have a better feel for the material and will be better able to guide the students through the lesson.

- Make sure that all of the participants have both an *In Search of Timothy* textbook and workbook.

- Participants will receive more from the videos and workbook if they do the reading assignment in the textbook ahead of time. Please encourage this.

- While a session could be done in less time, it is recommended that you have at least one hour allotted for each session. Each video lesson is approximately 28 minutes long. This leaves some time for going through the workbook together and for group interaction.

- It is helpful, after watching the video, to go through the Scenic Route and Inspection Station sections as a group and make sure people have grasped the material. You can ask different ones to provide answers throughout this review. Remember that having the right idea or concept is more important than having the exact right word.

- Next, it's good to have the group members share their reflections and thoughts from the Unpacking the Principles section. If you have a large number of people in the group, it can be helpful to have them break up into smaller groups of 5–6 members at this time.

To obtain additional *In Search of Timothy* textbooks or workbooks, please contact Faith Library Publications at 1-866-312-0972 or visit our Web site **www.rhema.org/store**. We also encourage you to visit Tony Cooke's Web site at **www.tonycooke.org.**

# Lesson 1

## Packing for the Trip

🚗 Read the preface and introduction from the textbook, *In Search of Timothy*

🚗 Watch Lesson 1 on DVD

🚗 Work through this chapter in the workbook

 ## The Expressway

In this lesson, Tony shares about his journey in "supportive ministry." Teamwork in the church is a major emphasis of these lessons–teamwork with God, the pastor, and each other. A church analyst is quoted regarding his experience in observing different church staffs, and it's not pretty.

A little background on Timothy in the Bible: Timothy is best known for the way he served and assisted the Apostle Paul. Pastors everywhere are looking for dependable, faithful people who have the same kind of servant's heart that Timothy had.

We learned from the Tower of Babel that when people are truly unified around a common goal, nothing is impossible to them. When God wants to do something in the earth, He raises up a leader and gives him or her a vision (a mental picture of a preferred future). He then surrounds that leader with others whose gifts and abilities can contribute to the fulfilling of God's purpose. God will reward us based on our faithfulness, not the visibility or glamour of what we do.

# The Scenic Route

1. This material is designed to teach _____ how to be better leaders, to teach followers how to be better followers, and to help each participant find and fulfill his or her place in the church.

2. Jesus is _____ to the church. He said, *". . . I will build My church, and the gates of Hades shall not prevail against it"* (Matt. 16:18).

3. This lesson is about teamwork. There are three key dimensions of the ones with whom we need to be in teamwork. We must be:

   • in teamwork with _____;

   • in teamwork with the _____; and

   • in teamwork with _____.

4. Satan does not want the Body of Christ to be in _____. He wants there to be division. He wants Christians to be spectators. He does not want a body of believers to recognize their gifts and callings and then put them into action, serving together to make a difference. When that happens, the Body of Christ will be very strong and the work of the enemy will be greatly hindered and minimized.

## Historical Marker

*"The hardest instrument in the orchestra to play is second fiddle."*

–Leonard Bernstein

5. The term, "supportive minister" is used in this lesson. Define what these two words mean and how they apply to us as members of the Body of Christ.

Supportive: _____
_____
_____

Minister: _____
_____
_____

## FUEL STOP

**Ephesians 4:11–12**

11 And He Himself gave . . . some pastors and teachers,

12 for the equipping of the saints for the work of ministry, for the edifying of the body of Christ.

6. What this means to the Body of Christ:_____

_____

_____

### Historical Marker

*"There is no more noble occupation in the world than to assist another human being—to help someone succeed."*

–Alan Loy McGinnis

7. Timothy is well known in Scripture for being a servant and an assistant to the Apostle Paul. Most everything we know about Timothy is in the context of how he helped, undergirded, supported, and lent strength to Paul's ministry. He was a partner, coworker, and co-laborer. There's no indication that Timothy was concerned about what kind of _____, position, or recognition he had.

"Pastors across the country and around the world are desperately searching for people who have a heart like Timothy. Pastors are yearning and longing to find individuals who are willing to come along side of them, and serve and partner with them in working for the Kingdom of God. A 'Timothy' is someone who is dependable, reliable, trustworthy, and faithful. Pastors all over the world are searching for Timothys."

8. Timothy was never meant to be enshrined as an isolated _____ of servitude in Scripture. He is a great pattern for every believer to follow and emulate as we endeavor to become the supportive ministers that God wants us to become.

"One of the things that made Timothy so outstanding was the level and degree of harmony and unity with which he walked in partnership with the Apostle Paul. Unity is something that is absolutely essential to the plan and purpose of God to be fulfilled."

9. What do we learn from the Tower of Babel about people—even those who are not serving a godly purpose? _____

_____

_____

_____

_____

### FUEL STOP

**Matthew 25:21**

*21 "His lord said to him, 'Well done, good and faithful servant; you were faithful over a few things, I will make you ruler over many things. Enter into the joy of your lord.'"*

> "Satan understands the unity principle, and that's why he works so hard to keep believers in the flesh; to keep believers carnal; to keep believers irritated with one another; to keep believers focusing on the petty, peripheral issues that really don't make any difference one way or the other. That's why Satan fights so hard to keep us from fully realizing what God's plan and purpose is, because if we ever get together on this thing, nothing's going to be impossible to us."

## Historical Marker

> "*I* am a member of a team, and I rely on the team, I defer to it and sacrifice for it, because the team, not the individual, is the ultimate champion."
>
> –Mia Hamm

10. Describe God's typical pattern when He wants to do something in the earth.

    First, He raises up a _____. Give some examples: _____
    _____
    _____

    Second, He gives that person a _____. Give the definition of that: _____
    _____
    _____

    Third, as the leader realizes the vision is bigger than he or she is, God responds by saying: "_____will be with you." That's natural help. "I will bring_____ to help you."

> "The art of leadership involves knowing where we are, seeing where we need to be, and then having the wisdom to take steps to get there and bring some other people along in the process."

## FUEL STOP

**1 Peter 4:10**
10 As each one has received a gift, minister it to one another, as good stewards of the manifold grace of God.

11. God never meant for His leaders to do all of the work _____. God never meant for His leaders to do the work without first receiving divine assistance in the spiritual realm; and secondly, natural help from people—those who are willing to become partners in the work. Sometimes people are quick to forget the contributions of those in what we might call secondary positions or supportive roles, or what the Bible calls in First Corinthians 12:28, the ministry of _____.

12. It is the contributions of individuals behind the scenes that very often make the difference between _____ and _____. Every spiritual leader today will tell you that without the help and assistance of a great number of people in the ministry of helps and supportive ministry, the reach, effectiveness, and impact of their ministry would be greatly _____.

 # Inspection Station

1. The church analyst Tony quoted was:

   a. Blessed by how many church leadership teams got along so well

   b. Discouraged by how poorly church leadership teams functioned in terms of harmony and unity

   c. Not expecting church leadership teams to get along any better than secular work teams

   d. Not concerned about problems because he felt that unity was not an important issue

   e. None of the above

2. The purpose of the pastor and the top leadership of the church is to:

   a. Serve as figureheads without necessarily having any real function

   b. Be performers and entertainers

   c. Do all of the work that needs to be done

   d. Equip believers so that everyone can be involved in getting the work done

   e. Both b and c above

3. Those who receive the greatest rewards in heaven will be:

   a. Those who had the most highly visible ministries

   b. Those who were on Christian television regularly

   c. Those who were the most faithful to serve

   d. Those who lived in the first century

   e. Both a and b above

 **Historical Marker**

> "*Snowflakes are one of nature's most fragile things, but just look at what they can do when they stick together.*"
>
> —Vesta M. Kelly

4. Which spiritual leader told God, as an excuse, *"...I am not eloquent ... but I am slow of speech and slow of tongue"* when he was called?

    a. Noah

    b. Moses

    c. Gideon

    d. Jeremiah

    e. Peter

### Historical Marker

*"The mark of a saint is not perfection, but consecration. A saint is not a man without faults, but a man who has given himself without reserve to God."*

–W.T. Richardson

5. Which spiritual leader told God, as an excuse, *"...O my Lord, how can I save Israel? Indeed my clan is the weakest in Manasseh, and I am the least in my father's house"* when he was called?

    a. Noah

    b. Moses

    c. Gideon

    d. Jeremiah

    e. Peter

### FUEL STOP

**Hebrews 10:24–25 (Amplified)**

24 And let us consider and give attentive, continuous care to watching over one another, studying how we may stir up (stimulate and incite) to love and helpful deeds and noble activities,

25 Not forsaking or neglecting to assemble together [as believers], as is the habit of some people, but admonishing (warning, urging, and encouraging) one another, and all the more faithfully as you see the day approaching.

6. Which spiritual leader told God, as an excuse, *"Ah, Lord God! Behold, I cannot speak, for I am a youth"* when he was called?

    a. Noah

    b. Moses

    c. Gideon

    d. Jeremiah

    e. Peter

## Unpacking the Principles

1. Why is the unity of a church leadership team so essential, and what effect does it (the unity or lack thereof) have on an entire congregation?

2. While there's nothing wrong with the word "staff," why did Tony prefer to use the term "supportive minister" rather than "staff member" for this seminar?

3. Timothy is well known in Scripture for what? Describe what you know about Timothy's attitude and function.

4. Does this statement bear witness with your heart? What does it mean to you? *"The Holy Spirit is searching across the land to find people who are not interested in prestige, not interested in recognition, not interested in fame, titles, or position, but people who are willing to work and to serve. I want you to join with the Holy Spirit in searching your own heart during this time of training. Ask yourself the question: 'Is God wanting me to be something that maybe I've not engaged in up to this point, or maybe not to the level or quality to which God has really called me to do it?'"*

**Matthew 16:18**

18 . . . I will build My church, and the gates of Hades shall not prevail against it.

5. Review the scriptures in this chapter listed as Fuel Stops. Which one speaks the most to you about where you are in your walk with and service toward God? Why?

6. Review the quotes in this chapter listed as Historical Markers. Which one is the most meaningful to you? Why?

7. What is one thing you learned from this lesson that you can apply to your life? How can it enhance the way you serve?

 ## Off Road

Acts 16:1–3

1 Then he [Paul] came to Derbe and Lystra. And behold, a certain disciple was there, named Timothy, the son of a certain Jewish woman who believed, but his father was Greek.

2 He was well spoken of by the brethren who were at Lystra and Iconium.

3 Paul wanted to have him go on with him. And he took him and circumcised him because of the Jews who were in that region, for they all knew that his father was Greek.

It is very likely that Paul personally led Timothy to the Lord on a previous visit to that region. He referred to him with these terms of paternal endearment:

- "*. . . my beloved and faithful son in the Lord . . .*" (1 Cor. 4:17).

- "*Timothy, a true son in the faith . . .*" (1 Tim. 1:2).

- "*Timothy, a beloved son . . .*" (2 Tim. 1:2).

We first meet Timothy in Acts 16, when Paul was ministering in Derbe and Lystra. It was earlier in Lystra (Acts 14:19) that Paul was stoned for having preached the Gospel and was dragged out of town, presumed to be dead.

For Timothy, associating himself with Paul was not necessarily the safest thing for him to do. When you are a partner with a "target," you can easily become a target yourself. Timothy knew that he was risking much to become connected with Paul.

And joining Paul's team was no small task. Paul knew that Timothy—because his mother was Jewish and his father was a Greek—would be an offense to the Jews because he was still uncircumcised. Timothy didn't need to be circumcised to be saved. The conference in Acts 15 had settled that issue. Circumcision was not something that was for Timothy's personal benefit, but rather, was done to not hinder ministry toward the Jews.

What is the lesson here? *There is a price you pay to be effective that you don't have to pay to be saved. There is a price you pay to be a distributor that you don't have to pay to be a consumer.* Timothy was willing to do whatever it took to increase his effectiveness in ministry. He understood that sacrifice was a part of serving God. What would happen today if to join a church staff or a volunteer team, one of the requirements was that every person had to go through a minor surgical procedure with no anesthetic? Do you think we'd have fewer people signing up to work in the church?

**FUEL STOP**

**1 Corinthians 1:10**

10 Now I plead with you, brethren, by the name of our Lord Jesus Christ, that you all speak the same thing , and that there be no divisions among you, but that you be perfectly joined together in the same mind and in the same judgment.

While circumcision may not be an issue today, are there still sacrifices that we have to make in order to meet the needs of others? Are there personal comforts or preferences that we relinquish in order to serve others more effectively?

# Travelogue

# Travelogue

# Lesson 2

## Packing for the Trip

🚐 In the textbook, *In Search of Timothy*, read

- The introduction to Part I

- Chapter 1, "The Challenges of Leadership"

- The first half of Chapter 2, "The Voices of Lonely Leaders" through the section titled, "No One Else Like Timothy"

🚐 Watch Lesson 2 on DVD

🚐 Work through this chapter in the workbook

## The Expressway

God doesn't want leaders to do their work alone. He helps them by raising up people to assist them with their gifts, talents, and abilities. Tony introduced the case studies of two leaders and their experiences in leadership.

Spiritual Leader #1 had a wonderful congregation, but experienced a painful split when a top assistant tried to take over. Spiritual Leader #1 later started a second congregation in another location, but that small group rejected the leader's influence.

Spiritual Leader #2 was a relative of the first leader. He was a great preacher and teacher, but had trouble retaining members of the congregation. There were also staff problems (jealousy, competition, and so forth.). One staff member committed assault with a deadly weapon, and another embezzled ministry funds. These were "follower-ship" problems, not problems of leadership.

The Apostle Paul experienced problems in his ministry as well. People deserted and abandoned him, but Paul found great comfort and assistance in the faithfulness of Timothy. Moses was another leader who found it to be lonely at the top. He discovered that he needed the help of others and had to learn not to do everything himself.

 **Historical Marker**

*"No employer today is independent of those about him. He cannot succeed alone, no matter how great his ability or capital. Business today is more than ever a question of cooperation."*

—Orison Swett Marden

 **The Scenic Route**

Case Studies in Leadership

1. Spiritual Leader #1

   a) Great character; great leader.

   b) Had a large congregation that appeared to be the most wonderful, ideal, and unified congregation that any spiritual leader could ever have. It seemed like the perfect scenario.

   c) One day, one of the top _____ in this congregation decided that he should be in charge—that he could do a better job than Spiritual Leader #1.

   d) A power play followed. Politicking, an insurrection, mutiny, rebellion, and an attempted overthrow of this spiritual leader.

   e) The rebellion wasn't strong enough to overthrow Spiritual Leader #1, but it created a very difficult rift in the congregation. This assistant ended up pulling away more than _____ of the congregation and gathered them around himself.

   f) The damage was done; a split occurred. But Spiritual Leader #1 continued to provide good leadership and do the best he could with his remaining congregation.

 **FUEL STOP**

**Exodus 18:17–18**

17 So Moses' father-in-law said to him, "The thing that you do is not good.

18 Both you and these people who are with you will surely wear yourselves out. For this thing is too much for you; you are not able to perform it by yourself."

g) Later, Spiritual Leader #1 "planted" an additional work in a new location.

h) In spite of his good intentions, the entire congregation soon turned against the founder. It was a very small work, but Spiritual Leader #1 lost the entire congregation.

i) Spiritual Leader #1 reached out again in an attempt to bring them back. He tried to reinfluence them and regather them. But they rejected his offers and he ended up being on the outside looking in. When he reached out, he was typically rejected.

## Historical Marker

*"Hold yourself responsible for a higher standard than anyone else expects of you. Never excuse yourself."*

–Henry Ward Beecher

j) After a long time and through a lot of blood, sweat, and tears, he was able to reconnect with that group and began to regather some of them and rebuild this congregation into a stronger, larger work. But it was a difficult process.

2. Spiritual Leader #2

a) A close _____ of Spiritual Leader #1. Spiritual Leader #2 also felt called into ministry.

b) Had a wonderful experience with the Holy Spirit and was anointed to preach. He became a dynamic preacher and a very gifted teacher. He had a great shepherd's heart. Even healings took place. People were greatly blessed by his ministry.

c) Spiritual Leader #2 was able to draw and attract large crowds, but he couldn't keep large crowds. He had retention problems and there was much turnover in his organization. That is, people would come to meetings but he couldn't keep them in the congregation.

d) Some of his top staff members did not get along with each other. There was much quarreling, strife, jealousy, division, and competition.

e) In a public setting his top assistant lost his cool and physically assaulted a member of the community and could have been charged with assault with a deadly weapon. Many people in the community witnessed the assault. Spiritual Leader #2 patched things up as best he could, but the situation was not good.

f) Another assistant was found guilty of financial impropriety. He was embezzling ministry funds for personal use.

## FUEL STOP

**John 6:66–67**

66 From that time many of His disciples went back and walked with Him no more.

67 Then Jesus said to the twelve, "Do you also want to go away?"

3. Spiritual Leader #1 is _____.

4. Spiritual Leader #2 is _____.

5. Spiritual Leader #1's original congregation was comprised of _____.

6. The assistant who tried to overthrow Spiritual Leader #1 is _____.

7. The two original members of Spiritual Leader #1's "second" congregation were _____ and _____.

8. The "staff members" of Spiritual Leader #2 who did not get along well with each other are _____.

9. The top assistant to Spiritual Leader #2 who committed assault with a deadly weapon is _____.

10. The other assistant to Spiritual Leader #2 who was guilty of embezzlement is _____.

11. God the Father and Jesus were both _____ leaders.

12. The problems that God and Jesus experienced in leadership were not really leadership problems; they were _____ problems.

## Historical Marker

> *"It marks a big step in your development when you come to realize that other people can help you do a better job than you could do alone."*
>
> –Andrew Carnegie

## FUEL STOP

**Philippians 3:12**

12 Not that I have already attained, or am already perfected; but I press on, that I may lay hold of that for which Christ Jesus has also laid hold of me.

"Good leadership doesn't work—at least not to its optimum level—without good follower-ship. It's not all on the leader's shoulders. Yes, leaders have a huge responsibility. Yes, leaders have tremendous potential and great opportunities for influence, but good leadership doesn't work to its optimum potential without the partnership of good followers."

"Paul had the fortitude, the courage, and reliance upon God to stand on his own when he had to, but he certainly liked to have partnership when he could and when it was available. But partnership wasn't always something Paul could control. He couldn't control the fact that all of his companions from Asia had deserted him. He couldn't control the fact that Demas had forsaken him. He couldn't control the fact that—at his first defense—nobody stood with him. Instead, everyone forsook him. He couldn't control those things, but he didn't hesitate to call out for Timothy: 'Timothy, come help me. Timothy, I need the books. Timothy, I need my coat.' He was looking for the aid and assistance of a partner who really had a heart to help."

 **Inspection Station**

1. Which of the following were components of Paul's life and ministry?

    a. The outstanding revelation, wisdom, insight, and understanding he received from the Lord

    b. The epistles he wrote that are now part of the New Testament

    c. The churches he started and the staggering persecutions he underwent

    d. The sense of aloneness and lack of support he sometimes experienced in ministry

    e. All of the above

2. Paul made three references in Second Timothy–the last epistle he wrote–to having been forsaken, abandoned, and so forth. Which of the following is *not* true relative to those statements?

    a. In spite of these abandonments by his friends, Paul was quick to point out that the Lord stood with him.

    b. Paul was looking for companionship, camaraderie, and teamwork in doing the work of the Lord.

    c. Paul was full of self-pity and felt sorry for himself.

    d. He acknowledged that Luke was still with him and called upon Timothy to come to him.

    e. None of the above. They are all true statements.

3. Which of the following are true statements about Paul's correspondence to the church at Philippi?

    a. Paul wrote the book of Philippians from a prison in Rome. Rome was in Italy, and Philippi was in northern Greece. Distance and communication were both big problems.

    b. Paul was deeply concerned about the welfare of all of the churches he started. He was concerned about the influence of false teachers and false doctrines. He was concerned that believers might fall away from God.

 **Historical Marker**

"*Every disciple needs three types of relationships in his life. He needs a 'Paul' who can mentor him and challenge him. He needs a 'Barnabas' who can come along side and encourage him. And he needs a 'Timothy,' someone that he can pour his life into.*"

–Dr. Howard Hendricks

c.  Because of Paul's limitations and restrictions (from being in prison), he needed someone who would go to Philippi on his behalf and serve as a bridge between him and the church there. He needed someone who would go as his representative—not his replacement. Someone who would go as an extension of his ministry and as an expression of his heart.

d.  All of the above

## Historical Marker

*"The body of every organization is structured from four kinds of bones. There are the wishbones, who spend all their time wishing someone would do the work. Then there are the jawbones, who do all the talking, but little else. The knucklebones knock everything anybody else tries to do. Fortunately, in every organization there are also the backbones, who get under the load and do most of the work."*

–Leo Aikman

# Unpacking the Principles

1.  What do you think of the old saying, "It's lonely at the top"? How did that apply in the lives of great leaders in the Bible, and how does it apply in the lives of spiritual leaders today? What can other members of the body of Christ do to minimize or eliminate this problem?

2.  Paul said, *". . . Demas has forsaken me, having loved this present world . . ."* (2 Tim. 4:10). What affect can this have on spiritual leaders and on others in the body of Christ, even the morale of a local church? What is the correct way for leaders and others to process such choices by others?

3.  When Timothy went to Philippi on Paul's behalf, he went as Paul's representative. What is the difference between Timothy going as Paul's *representative* as opposed to going as his *replacement*? What is the difference between Timothy going as an *extension* of Paul as opposed to going as his *substitute*?

4.  If Paul was such a great leader, what might be some of the reasons why he didn't seem to have many committed followers (at least at certain times)?

5.  Read Exodus 18:13–26. What was the problem? What solution did Jethro (Moses' father-in-law) propose?

6.  Review the scriptures in the Fuel Stops. Which one speaks the most to you about where you are in your walk with and service toward God? Why?

## FUEL STOP

**Philippians 2:19–21**

19 But I trust in the Lord Jesus to send Timothy to you shortly, that I also may be encouraged when I know your state.

20 For I have no one like-minded, who will sincerely care for your state.

21 For all seek their own, not the things which are of Christ Jesus.

7. Review the quotes in the Historical Markers. Which one is the most meaningful to you? Why?

8. What is one thing you learned from this lesson that you can apply to your life? How can it enhance the way you serve?

## FUEL STOP

**Romans 1:11–12**

11 For I long to see you, that I may impart to you some spiritual gift, so that you may be established—

12 that is, that I may be encouraged together with you by the mutual faith both of you and me.

# Off Road

The Bricklayer: Trying to Do the Job Alone
Author Unknown

Dear Sir:

I am writing in response to your request for additional information for my insurance claim. In block number three of the accident claim form I wrote, "trying to do the job alone" as the cause of my accident. You said in your letter that I should explain that statement more fully. I trust the following details will be sufficient.

I am a bricklayer by trade. On the date of the accident, I was working alone on the roof of a new six-story building. When I completed my work, I discovered that I had about 500 pounds of brick left over. Rather than carrying the bricks down by hand, I decided to lower them in a barrel by using a pulley that was attached to the side of the building at the sixth-floor level.

# Historical Marker

*"Trust in yourself, and you are doomed to disappointment. Trust in your friends and they will die and leave you. Trust in money and you may have it taken away from you. Trust in reputation and some slanderous tongues will blast it. But trust in God and you are never to be confounded in time or in eternity."*

—Dwight L. Moody

Securing the rope at ground level, I went up to the roof, swung the barrel out, and loaded the bricks into it. Then I went back to the ground and untied the rope, holding it tightly to insure a slow descent of the 500 pounds of bricks. You will note in block number 22 of the claim form that my weight is 150 pounds.

Due to my surprise at being jerked off the ground so suddenly, I lost my presence of mind and forgot to let go of the rope. Needless to say, I proceeded up the side of the building at a very rapid rate of speed.

In the vicinity of the third floor, I met the barrel coming down. This explains my fractured skull and collarbone. Slowed only slightly, I continued my rapid ascent, not stopping until the fingers of my right hand were two knuckles deep into the pulley.

By this time, I regained my presence of mind and was able to hold tightly to the rope in spite of my pain. At approximately the same time however, the barrel of bricks hit the ground and the bottom fell out of the barrel. Devoid of the weight of the bricks, the barrel then weighed approximately 50 pounds.

I refer you again to the information in block number 22 regarding my weight. As you might imagine, I began a rapid descent down the side of the building. In the vicinity of the third floor, I met the barrel coming up. This accounts for the two fractured ankles and the lacerations of my legs and lower body.

This second encounter with the barrel slowed me enough to lessen my injuries when I fell onto the pile of bricks, and fortunately, only three vertebrae were cracked.

I am sorry to report, however, that as I lay there on the bricks in pain, unable to stand, and watching the empty barrel six stories above me, I again lost my presence of mind, and let go of the rope. The empty barrel weighed more than the rope so it came down upon me and broke both of my legs.

I hope I have furnished information sufficient to explain why "trying to do the job alone" was the stated cause of the accident.

Sincerely,

A Bricklayer

 **Historical Marker**

*"In the spiritual realm, a man who will lead a rebellion has already proven, no matter how grandiose his words or angelic his ways, that he has a critical nature, an unprincipled character, and hidden motives in his heart. Frankly, he is a thief. He creates dissatisfaction and tension within the realm, and then either seizes power or siphons off followers. The followers he gets, he uses to found his own dominion. Such a sorry beginning, built on the foundation of insurrection . . . No, God never honors division in His realm. I find it curious that men who feel qualified to split God's kingdom do not feel capable of going somewhere else, to another land, to raise up a completely new kingdom. No, they must steal from another leader. I have never seen the exception. They seem always to need at least a few pre-packaged followers."*[1]

—Gene Edwards

# Travelogue

# Travelogue

# Lesson 3

## Packing for the Trip

🚗 In the textbook, *In Search of Timothy*, read

- The remainder of Chapter 2, "The Voices of Lonely Leaders" beginning with the section titled "Moses: A Do-It-Yourself Kind of Guy"

- The beginning of Chapter 3, "Learning to Be Like Timothy" through the section titled "Correction #1: Be Faithful in the 'Little' "

🚗 Watch Lesson 3 on DVD

🚗 Work through this chapter in the workbook

## The Expressway

Moses learned, with the help of his father-in-law, to delegate. Men of godly character helped him carry the burden of governing the Israelites. Even though the structure was put into place, Moses didn't necessarily let go—spiritually or emotionally—of the burden of the people.

Later, God took the Spirit that was on Moses and placed it on the selected leaders so they could help him. This was not to lessen Moses' role in leadership, but to create partnerships through which his leadership could be carried out. Actually, Moses, Elijah, Jesus, and Paul often felt alone and unsupported as they carried out their missions. We can't go back and help *those* leaders, but we can help and support the leaders in our midst.

Tony shared the frustrations and challenges he faced as a church janitor and the attitude problems that ensued. He faced anger, jealousy, a critical attitude, and apathy, but the Lord began to deal with him about these things and helped him learn to serve with a right attitude.

## Historical Marker

*"Whatever you are, be a good one."*
–Abraham Lincoln

# The Scenic Route

1. Instead of Moses doing all the work, _____ encouraged Moses to set up a system involving the _____ of responsibilities.

2. The gist of the system that Jethro encouraged was that the leaders under Moses would handle all the _____ things, and only the more _____ things would be brought to Moses (Exod. 18:22).

3. Jethro indicated that there were benefits to delegating. He told Moses (Exod. 18:22b–23):

   22 ". . . So it will be _____ for you, for they will bear the burden with you.
   23 If you do this thing, and God so commands you, then you will be able to _____, and all this people will also go to their place in peace."

4. We assume that Moses went ahead and set up a system of delegation, but he may have never spiritually or emotionally released the responsibilities. As a result, he ended up saying to God in Numbers 11:11, ". . . *Why have You _____ Your servant? And why have I not found favor in Your sight, that You have laid the _____ of all these people on me?*

5. Elijah also became overwhelmed and felt alone in his work. Like Moses, he also expressed a desire to _____ (1 Kings 19:4).

## FUEL STOP

**Matthew 10:8**

8 . . . Freely you have received, freely give.

"In reading the accounts of what Jesus experienced in the Garden of Gethsemane, we see that He underwent something so deep and profound that we can neither comprehend nor express it in words. Jesus experienced soul anguish. He asked Peter, James, and John to come with Him into the garden a little bit further. When Jesus began to pray, He was in great anguish and was very distraught. What were Peter, James, and John doing? They were sleeping. Jesus kept going back to them and saying, 'Couldn't you watch with me one hour? Couldn't you just be with me?' In His humanity, Jesus was feeling emotions that humans feel. He was feeling despair; He was feeling loneliness; He was feeling dread of what was about to happen. And Jesus was looking for the comfort and consolation that could only come through companionship. Yet, His closest friends slept through almost the entire experience."

6. While we can't help Moses, Elijah, Jesus (in His earthly ministry), or Paul, what can we do? _____
_____
_____
_____

### Historical Marker

"*If* a man is called to be a street sweeper, he should sweep streets even as Michelangelo painted, or Beethoven composed music, or Shakespeare wrote poetry. He should sweep streets so well that all the hosts of heaven and earth will pause to say, 'Here lived a great street sweeper who did his job well.' "

–Martin Luther King Jr.

7. We're not simply called to be _____ of blessing, but we're called to be _____ of blessing. We're called to be channels and vessels of blessings for others, and we're all called to have our life transformed so that we can truly be the kind of servant that Timothy was.

8. As a janitor, Tony went from praying, "God _____ me," to complaining, "God, they're _____ me."

9. Sometimes we want the Lord to speak to us, but we want Him to say what we _____ Him to say, not necessarily what we _____ to hear.

### FUEL STOP

**Luke 16:10–12 (NIV)**

10 "Whoever can be trusted with very little can also be trusted with much, and whoever is dishonest with very little will also be dishonest with much.

11 So if you have not been trustworthy in handling worldly wealth, who will trust you with true riches?

12 And if you have not been trustworthy with someone else's property, who will give you property of your own?

10. The correction Tony received from the Lord was, "I want you to treat this job as though it was your ultimate calling and as though it was the most _____ thing you could ever do for Me."

# Inspection Station

1. When Moses was on the verge of being overworked (Exod. 18), he received instruction by way of:

    a. God speaking out of a burning bush

    b. God giving him a vision

    c. Advice from his father-in-law

    d. An angelic appearance

    e. All of the above

2. What specific issues did Jethro identify about the way Moses had been doing things?

    a. The thing you're doing is not good.

    b. You're going to wear yourself and the people out.

    c. The load is too much for you.

    d. You are not able to do it all by yourself.

    e. All of the above

3. What were the qualifications that Moses was instructed to look for in the men he chose to help him (Exod. 18)?

    a. Able men

    b. Men that fear God

    c. Men of truth

    d. Men that hate covetousness

    e. All of the above

## FUEL STOP

**Exodus 18:13–23**

13 And so it was, on the next day, that Moses sat to judge the people; and the people stood before Moses from morning until evening.

14 So when Moses' father-in-law saw all that he did for the people, he said, "What is this thing that you are doing for the people? Why do you alone sit, and all the people stand before you from morning until evening?"

15 And Moses said to his father-in-law, "Because the people come to me to inquire of God.

16 When they have a difficulty, they come to me, and I judge between one and another; and I make known the statutes of God and His laws."

17 So Moses' father-in-law said to him, "The thing that you do is not good.

18 Both you and these people who are with you will surely wear yourselves out. For this thing is too much for you; you are not able to perform it by yourself.

19 Listen now to my voice; I will give you counsel, and God will be with you: Stand before God for the people, so that you may bring the difficulties to God.

20 And you shall teach them the statutes and the laws, and show them the way in which they must walk and the work they must do.

21 Moreover you shall select from all the people able men, such as fear God, men of truth, hating covetousness; and place such over them to be rulers of thousands, rulers of hundreds, rulers of fifties, and rulers of tens.

22 And let them judge the people at all times. Then it will be that every great matter they shall bring to you, but every small matter they themselves shall judge. So it will be easier for you, for they will bear the burden with you.

23 If you do this thing, and God so commands you, then you will be able to endure, and all this people will also go to their place in peace."

# Unpacking the Principles

1. Peter, James, and John slept through some of their most important training opportunities. Can we as believers "sleep" through some of the opportunities we have? What can we do about that?

2. It's safe to assume that Timothy grew and developed in the characteristics that made him such a beneficial servant and assistant to the Apostle Paul. How do you feel about your growth and development? In what areas have you grown the most? In what areas do you still need the most work?

3. Has God ever had you serve in an area that you didn't feel was your "ultimate calling?" How did you do with that?

4. Have you ever received correction from God about an attitude issue, only to have the same bad attitude resurface later? Is there any particular attitude challenge you deal with that seems to be especially persistent?

 **Historical Marker**

> "*Somehow ungodly men have developed systems of organization which permit them to work together in states of relative harmony and unity, whereas godly men, refusing to admit that these organizational structures are needed, live in states of chaos and disunity. The tragedy of this fact becomes evident when we realize that many of the successful systems of organization under which the ungodly men work and which the godly men refuse to accept are biblically based.*"
>
> —Ted W. Engstrom and R. Alec Mackenzie

## FUEL STOP

**Numbers 11:11–12, 14–15**

11 So Moses said to the Lord, "Why have You afflicted Your servant? And why have I not found favor in Your sight, that You have laid the burden of all these people on me?

12 Did I conceive all these people? Did I beget them, that You should say to me, 'Carry them in your bosom, as a guardian carries a nursing child,' to the land which You swore to their fathers?

14 I am not able to bear all these people alone, because the burden is too heavy for me.

15 If You treat me like this, please kill me here and now—if I have found favor in Your sight—and do not let me see my wretchedness!"

5. Review the scriptures in the Fuel Stops. Which one speaks the most to you about where you are in your walk with and service toward God? Why?

6. Review the quotes in the Historical Markers. Which one is the most meaningful to you? Why?

7. What is one thing you learned from this lesson that you can apply to your life? How can it enhance the way you serve?

# Off Road

**Do You Have a "Disciple" or a "Church" Mentality?**

Have you ever considered how the words *disciple* and *church* are used throughout the New Testament? We know that both of these are good words, but the frequency and ratio with which they are used as the New Testament progresses is very interesting.

In the Gospels, the word *church* appears only three times, while *disciple* and *disciples* appear 242 times. That's a lopsided ratio. In the Book of Acts, things balance out a bit. *Church* and *churches* are used 20 times, while *disciple* and *disciples* are used 32 times. There's a dramatic shift in the other direction, though, when we move into the Epistles and the Book of Revelation. There, *church* and *churches* are used 87 times, and *disciple* and *disciples* are not used a single time.

Is there significance in this changing ratio? I think there is. Here is one thought: A person could consider himself to be a disciple—a student, a learner, or pupil—on his own. If a person was stranded alone on a desert island with his Bible, he could learn about Jesus. However, he would still be lacking a spiritual community even though Jesus might be very precious to him.

A person can start out as a disciple of Jesus individually, but the farther he progresses in following the Lord and His teachings, the more he is going to be drawn to and integrated into the church—into vital, interdependent relationships with other believers. It's not that we lose our individual relationship with the Lord, as that will always be important. But the farther we go spiritually, the more the emphasis should be on *we*, not just on *me*.

Our personal relationship with God will always be vital and foundational, but that relationship will find enrichment, enhancement, and expression through mutually beneficial relationships with others in the Body of Christ. We can always profit from private time with God in prayer and study, but we should avoid excessive isolation from others. Can we know and love God individually? Certainly. But there is something very powerful about what

## Historical Marker

*"I long to accomplish a great and noble task, but it is my chief duty to accomplish small tasks as if they were great and noble."*

–Helen Keller

## FUEL STOP

**1 Kings 19:4, 10**

4 But he himself went a day's journey into the wilderness, and came and sat down under a broom tree. And he prayed that he might die, and said, "It is enough! Now, Lord, take my life, for I am no better than my fathers!"

10 So he [Elijah] said, "I have been very zealous for the Lord God of hosts; for the children of Israel have forsaken Your covenant, torn down Your altars, and killed Your prophets with the sword. I alone am left; and they seek to take my life."

David expressed in Psalm 34:3: *"Oh, magnify the Lord with me, And let us exalt His name together."*

Michael G. Moriarty expressed concern about the issue of excessive isolation when he said, "In evangelical individualism people think of their personal relationship with God in isolation ('Just me and Jesus') and forge their destiny apart from any church authority. While holding relatively low opinions of history, traditions, and the church, they turn to the experiences of self and isolate themselves from their brothers and sisters in the faith. True spirituality is perverted as it becomes a quest for inner stimulation rather than growth in biblical knowledge and the application of truth in community. Healthy Christians do not live in isolation."

## Historical Marker

*"We are what we repeatedly do. Excellence then, is not an act, but a habit."*

—Aristotle

## FUEL STOP

**1 Samuel 16:7**

7 "... For the Lord does not see as man sees; for man looks at the outward appearance, but the Lord looks at the heart."

We should do all that we can to promote partnership in the Body of Christ. In doing so, we will all benefit from the kind of teamwork that makes the dream work!

## Travelogue

# Travelogue

# Lesson 4

## Packing for the Trip

🚗 In the textbook, *In Search of Timothy*, read

- The remainder of Chapter 3, "Learning to Be Like Timothy" beginning with "Correction #2: Be That Person!"

- Chapter 4, "Four Commitments Supportive Ministers Must Make"

🚗 Watch Lesson 4 on DVD

🚗 Work through this chapter in the workbook

## The Expressway

Tony continued sharing how the Lord helped him to get rid of some wrong attitudes and establish right attitudes about serving. God doesn't just want us to do a good job externally, but He desires that we serve Him with a heart to glorify and please Him.

People don't evolve into great supportive ministers by accident; they have to develop, grow, and make the necessary commitments to becoming like Timothy. We must be committed to God and His Word, to His Church, to our own calling, and to the pastor for whom we work.

How dramatic one's call is isn't the most significant thing; what really matters is how faithful we are to what God puts in our hearts and to the opportunities He makes available to us.

# The Scenic Route

1. Excellence is not something we do when we reach some high level that we think is
   _____, but excellence begins with the seemingly _____
   things that are before us right now.

2. When Tony was harboring critical thoughts, he sensed the Lord asking him, "If you were
   the _____, what kind of janitor would you want working for you?"

   > "We can be at a place in our lives where we have the spiritual sensitivity to receive a word of correction, but
   > we lack the spiritual maturity and discipline to walk it out. That's where I was. I was spiritually sensitive
   > enough to receive correction, but I wasn't spiritually mature enough, or disciplined enough, to maintain
   > that correction in my walk over a period of time."

3. Tony said, "I was doing my job on the _____, but I was grumbling and complaining on the _____. It is possible to have outward compliance and, at the
   same time, be operating in inward rebellion."

## FUEL STOP

**Philippians 2:14** (Message)
14 Do everything readily and cheerfully—no
bickering, no second-guessing allowed!

4. The third correction Tony received was when
   the Holy Spirit spoke to his heart and said, "I
   want you to clean this restroom as though
   _____ Himself were the next
   person coming in here.

   > "Believers should be the hardest working employees, the hardest working volunteers, and the hardest
   > working leaders. We should be diligent and disciplined in our work because we are doing our work to
   > glorify and honor God."

## Historical Marker

5. I do not believe that people evolve into great supportive
   ministers by _____. Somebody is not
   successful just because he or she shows up, although
   showing up is a big part. People have to _____
   and grow into great supportive ministers.

   *"True heroism is remarkably sober, very
   undramatic. It is not the urge to surpass all
   others at whatever cost, but the urge to serve
   others at whatever the cost."*

   —Arthur Ashe

6. **Commitment #1:** We must be committed to
   _____ and His _____.

7. People can get so involved in church work and working
   *for* God that they forget to have a _____
   *with* God.

8. A position or a title in the church is never a _____ for personal or spiritual
   growth.

9. When Jesus called the twelve, He was not simply interested in their ministry
   _____. He was interested in their personal development and the
   _____ of their character.

10. **Commitment #2:** We need to be committed to the _____. People who love
    the Lord should love what He loves. They should love His people and hold them in the
    highest regard (in spite of their faults and flaws). The church is the body of Christ, and if
    we wouldn't do it to Jesus, we shouldn't do it to the church, in spite of any flaws or failures
    that might exist.

11. **Commitment #3:** We need to be committed to our own _____. Some
    people think that a calling only has to do with those who are called to _____.
    But we are all called; we are all called to serve. A few are called to serve behind the pulpit,
    but many more are called to serve behind the _____.

"Cleaning the toilets in the church is real ministry. And God values and honors it. When you understand
that what you are doing is for the Lord and for the furtherance of His church and the Gospel, then what you
are doing is a calling. It is an assignment from Heaven and it is real ministry. When you know it's a call,
when you know it's an assignment from Heaven, then that can be an anchor of stability in your life when
the going gets tough; when your flesh gets irritated; and when your flesh gets frustrated. When you know
it's a call from God, it will see you through the rough times; it will see you through the tough times."

It's not how dramatic and how dramatically you are called; it's how faithful you are in what
God makes available to you and what He put in your heart to do.

12. **Commitment #4:** We need to be committed to the
_____.

### Historical Marker

"*Do all the good you can, in all the ways
you can, to all the souls you can,
in every place you can, at all the times
you can, with all the zeal you can,
as long as you ever can.*"

–John Wesley

13. When we see different men and women throughout the
Bible that served in supportive roles, it doesn't mean
that they put the leaders on pedestals and worshipped
them. It wasn't some kind of ego exaltation, but rather,
it was a _____ of the call of God, the
plan of God, and the purpose of God.

## Inspection Station

1. Colossians 3:22–24 says that servants are to do their work:

   a. Not with eyeservice

   b. Not as men-pleasers

   c. In sincerity of heart, fearing God

   d. Heartily, as unto the Lord

   e. All of the above

2. The church that Jesus said in Revelation 2:4
   had "left their first love" was:

   a. The church at Laodicea

   b. The church at Smyrna

   c. The church at Antioch

   d. The church at Ephesus

   e. None of the above

### FUEL STOP

**Colossians 3:22–24**

22 Bondservants, obey in all things your masters
according to the flesh, not with eyeservice, as
men-pleasers, but in sincerity of heart, fearing God.

23 And whatever you do, do it heartily, as to the
Lord and not to men,

24 knowing that from the Lord you will receive the
reward of the inheritance; for you serve the Lord
Christ.

3. The first and foremost priority that Jesus had when He called and appointed the Twelve was that:

   a. They might be with Him

   b. That He might send them forth to preach

   c. That they might have power to heal sicknesses

   d. That they might cast out demons

   e. All of the above

 **Historical Marker**

> "*I found that the men and women who got to the top were those who did the jobs they had in hand, with everything they had of energy and enthusiasm and hard work.*"
>
> –Harry Truman

4. Which of the following is true of Jesus and the church?

   a. Jesus gave His life for the church.

   b. Jesus said, "I will build my church. . . ."

   c. Jesus loves the church.

   d. Jesus is coming back for a glorious church without spot, wrinkle, or any such thing.

   e. All of the above

5. Which of the following is *not* true as it pertains to the call of God?

   a. Different people have different ways of perceiving or experiencing the call of God on their lives.

   b. It is vital that our calling be dramatic and sensational. Those who are called through a dream, an audible voice, or an angelic appearance will always have the most effective ministries.

   c. What matters most is not the manner in which we are called, but that we are faithful and obedient to do those things that God puts in our heart.

   d. Most people who are called will simply have an inward witness, an inward knowing, or an inward desire to do something for God (as opposed to a spectacular experience).

   e. None of the above are untrue–they are all true statements.

 **FUEL STOP**

**Revelation 2:2–4**

2 "I know your works, your labor, your patience, and that you cannot bear those who are evil. And you have tested those who say they are apostles and are not, and have found them liars;

3 and you have persevered and have patience, and have labored for My name's sake and have not become weary.

4 Nevertheless I have this against you, that you have left your first love.

# Unpacking the Principles

1. How does "the Golden Rule" apply to our relationships in church? How does it apply in our attitude and actions toward those in leadership?

2. Are you the kind of church member you would desire to have if you were the pastor? In what ways?

3. Have you ever found yourself being so caught up in the work of ministry or serving that you neglected your personal relationship with the Lord? What did you do to remedy the situation?

### Historical Marker

*"Any fool can criticize, condemn, and complain, and most fools do."*

—Benjamin Franklin

## FUEL STOP

**Romans 12:6**

6 Having then gifts differing according to the grace that is given to us, let us use them. . . .

4. What do you think of this statement? "We shouldn't look at any area of serving as a stepping stone to something higher and better. If God happens to move you into something different that's fine, but whatever you are doing, treat it as important and give it your best."

5. What do you think of the statement Tony made relative to John 15:16, which states: *"You did not choose me, but I chose you. . . ."* "He chose you. You didn't *decide* to start serving God. If it was your choice, then you can do whatever you want to. But if it's God's call, then you're going to answer to Him, and you need to be faithful."

6. Review the scriptures in the Fuel Stops. Which one speaks the most to you about where you are in your walk with and service toward God? Why?

7. Review the quotes in the Historical Markers. Which one is the most meaningful to you? Why?

8. What is one thing you learned from this lesson that you can apply to your life? How can it enhance the way you serve?

### Historical Marker

*"Don't find fault, find a remedy; anybody can complain."*

—Henry Ford

 **Off Road**

## The Father and His Sons

*From Aesop's Fables*

A father had a family of sons who were perpetually quarreling among themselves. When he failed to heal their disputes by his exhortations, he determined to give them a practical illustration of the evils of disunion; and for this purpose he one day told them to bring him a bundle of sticks. When they had done so, he placed the bundle into the hands of each of them in succession, and ordered them to break it in pieces. They tried with all their strength, and were not able to do it.

He next opened the bundle, took the sticks separately, one by one, and again put them into his sons' hands, upon which they broke them easily. He then addressed them in these words: "My sons, if you are of one mind, and unite to assist each other, you will be as this bundle, uninjured by all the attempts of your enemies; but if you are divided among yourselves, you will be broken as easily as these sticks."

## Travelogue

_____

_____

_____

_____

_____

_____

_____

# Travelogue

# Lesson 5

## Packing for the Trip

🚗 In the textbook, *In Search of Timothy*, read

- Chapter 5, "Keeping Perspective by Keeping Priorities"

- The introduction to "Part II, Biblical Examples of Supportive Ministry"

- Chapter 6, "Paul and Timothy: Kindred Spirits"

🚗 Watch Lesson 5 on DVD

🚗 Work through this chapter in the workbook

 ## The Expressway

When God wants to do something in the earth, He will typically raise up a leader and give that leader an assignment or a "vision," a mental image or a spiritual picture of the way things could be or should be—a preferred future. That calling, assignment, or vision is always bigger than the leader, so God does two things: 1) He makes His anointing and ability available to that leader, and 2) He surrounds that leader with others who can help and assist.

When leadership and follower-ship work together in partnership, great things happen. It's not just pastors and missionaries who have a calling; every believer is called to serve God in some capacity. While a few are called to serve God behind the pulpit, many are called to serve God behind the scenes.

When we serve God in a supportive role, we need to have the right priorities and perspectives about our calling. First, we serve the purpose of God. Second, we respect the office that a leader stands in. Third, we learn to work with people's personalities. Every personality type has its strengths and weaknesses, and we need to work at bringing out the best in each other. Paul was diligent to bring out the best in Timothy, even though he was aware of Timothy's weaknesses.

**Historical Marker**

*"The counterfeit trinity is me, myself, and I."*
—Edwin Louis Cole

The session concluded with Tony teaching on six of the eight characteristics of Timothy from Philippians 2:19–22.

# The Scenic Route

1. When God wants to do something wonderful in the earth, He typically will raise up a _____. There are pastors and other ministry leaders all over the world that are endeavoring to carry out the _____ or assignment that God has given them.

2. It seems like Satan works overtime trying to bring division and strife into the church and turning people who have been active _____ into passive _____.

3. It's not simply pastors, evangelists, or missionaries who have a divine _____. God calls many of us to what is called _____ ministry. We all have a calling. We're not all called to serve behind the pulpit, but at least we are called to serve behind the _____.

4. Priorities and Perspectives for the Servant's Heart

   a. We are to serve the _____ of God.

   b. We are to respect the _____ in which the pastor stands.

   c. We are to learn to work with the _____ of the pastor.

5. Purpose will remain when personalities have _____ and gone. Personalities _____; the purpose of God does not.

6. When "excessive _____" occurs, people often have difficulty delineating different roles (i.e., respecting the office of the pastor versus simply knowing him as a "buddy").

7. Even though Saul behaved badly in the office of king and tried to kill David, David continued to refer to Saul as "the Lord's _____." Saul certainly wasn't acting like the Lord's anointed, but he still was in that office and David respected the office in which Saul stood.

> "Each personality type has its strengths and weaknesses, and in the body of Christ there is a wide variety of personalities. If we're not careful, our personalities can get on each other's nerves, and we can start to bring out the worst instead of the best in each other. If we're not careful, the carnality in you will bring out the carnality in me; or the carnality in me will bring out the carnality in you. But we want to bring out the best in each other, so we need to learn how to work with each other's personalities. Keep in mind that not only do you have to get along with your coworker's personality, but your coworker has to get along with your personality too."

8. The apostle Paul demonstrated patience and tolerance in working with young Timothy. This was necessary, because Timothy, in his personality, had some issues. Timothy had a tendency to become _____, to be intimidated, and was inclined to "pull back" at times. Even though Timothy had these tendencies, Paul encouraged Timothy in those matters and encouraged him to grow in those areas. He worked with Timothy and tried to cultivate and develop the right things in him.

> "A leader should aspire to be the kind of mentor that Paul was to Timothy. Followers should aspire to become as submitted, cooperative, loyal, and faithful as Timothy was to Paul. This would begin to form bonds of teamwork and partnership in ministry that would bring a great increase of effectiveness and productivity in churches and ministries."

9. One of the things that brings corruption and contamination to partnerships–instead of loyalty, unity, and teamwork–is when individuals have a personal _____.

**FUEL STOP**

**Ephesians 4:3** (Message)
3 . . . alert at noticing differences and quick at mending fences.

## Eight Characteristics of a Timothy

Philippians 2:19–22

19 But I trust in the Lord Jesus to send Timothy to you shortly, that I also may be encouraged when I know your state.

20 For I have no one like-minded, who will sincerely care for your state.

21 For all seek their own, not the things which are of Christ Jesus.

22 But you know his proven character, that as a son with his father he served with me in the gospel.

We'll cover six of the eight traits in this lesson. The last two points will be covered in the next lesson.

### Historical Marker

"*Could Hamlet have been written by a committee, or the Mona Lisa painted by a club? Could the New Testament have been composed as a conference report? Creative ideas do not spring from groups. They spring from individuals. The divine spark leaps from the finger of God to Adam.*"

–Alfred Whitney Griswold

1.  A Timothy is someone who inspires _____ in the heart of a leader.

    If Timothy had not been loyal, faithful, reliable, and dependable, he would not have inspired trust in Paul's heart.

2.  A Timothy is someone whose ministry and work _____ a spiritual leader.

    What happens when workers have not been loyal or dependable? What happens if they're up-and-down, erratic, and inconsistent? It causes a leader's heart to be _____ because things aren't being done well: they aren't done in quality; they aren't representing the church well; they aren't representing the Lord Jesus well—and that discourages a leader. But Paul said, "I trust in the Lord Jesus to send Timothy to you that I may be encouraged" (Phil. 2:19). He knew that Timothy's ministry would result in encouragement.

3.  A Timothy is someone who is _____ to a leader.

He provides an answer, or a report back to the leader. Paul said, "*. . . that I also may be encouraged when I know your state*" (Phil. 2:19). Timothy was not only going to go to the Philippians on Paul's behalf, but Timothy was going to come back and give a report to Paul. Timothy wasn't going on this assignment to do his own thing or to fulfill his own agenda. He was going there to represent Paul, and then he was going to come back to Paul because he was accountable to him.

### FUEL STOP

**Ephesians 4:2–3 (NLT)**

2 Always be humble and gentle. Be patient with each other, making allowance for each other's faults because of your love.

3 Make every effort to keep yourselves united in the Spirit, binding yourselves together with peace.

4. A Timothy is someone who is _____ minded.

   This word in the Greek is made up of two words in our language that mean *equal* _____. Timothy shared:

   - Paul's heart

   - Paul's vision

   - Paul's values

   - Paul's commitment

   - Paul's _____

5. A Timothy is someone who sincerely _____.

   A Timothy is not a _____, which is someone who's merely doing it for the money or the prestige. A Timothy is in it, first and foremost, because he cares.

6. A Timothy is someone who is not _____ seeking.

   Paul said, "*For all seek their own, not the things which are of Christ Jesus*" (Phil. 2:21). A Timothy is not trying to build his own kingdom or bring people to himself. A Timothy is someone who is willing to help build the leader's vision. He is not using his relationship to the leader to ultimately advance his own personal cause. A Timothy is someone who has truly made himself a supportive partner with another by stepping across the line of self-centeredness and self-seeking.

 **Inspection Station**

1. What typically happens when God raises up a leader and gives that leader an assignment?

   a. The leader realizes that the assignment is bigger than he or she is personally.

   b. The leader recognizes his or her need for God's help in the supernatural.

   c. The leader recognizes his or her need for the help of people in the natural.

   d. Great things happen when leadership and followers work together in partnership.

   e. All of the above

2. Which of the following statements is *not* true when it comes to purpose and personalities?

   a. We all have imperfect personalities, with quirks, flaws, and idiosyncrasies.

   b. We are to serve God based on His purpose; it is foundational and will remain steady when personality conflicts and other difficulties arise.

   c. Because of the sanctification and spirituality of all believers, it is likely that we will never be "rubbed the wrong way" by anyone else's personality or see anything in other believers or leaders that would disappoint us.

   d. Purpose transcends personalities.

   e. None of the above is false. They are all true statements.

3. Which of the following is true of Jesus' ministry in his hometown in Mark 6:2–6?

   a. They were astonished at Jesus' wisdom and works.

   b. They respected the office and ministry that God had given Jesus to fulfill.

   c. What they knew about him in the natural did not hinder their ability to receive from his ministry.

   d. Jesus indicated that prophets are respected equally in their hometown and in other places.

   e. All of the above

 **Historical Marker**

*"Teamwork is what the Green Bay Packers were all about. They didn't do it for individual glory. They did it because they loved one another."*

–Coach Vince Lombardi

4. Which of the following is true about getting along with each other according to various translations of Ephesians 4:2–3?

   a. We are to be humble and gentle toward one another.

   b. We need to make allowances for each other's faults because of our love.

   c. We are to make every effort to keep ourselves united in the Spirit.

   d. We are to be alert at noticing differences and quick at mending fences.

   e. All of the above

 **FUEL STOP**

**Ephesians 4:2–3 (KJV)**

2 With all lowliness and meekness, with longsuffering, forbearing one another in love;

3 Endeavoring to keep the unity of the Spirit in the bond of peace.

# Unpacking the Principles

1. In considering our priorities–serving the purpose of God, respecting the office someone stands in, and learning to work with the personalities involved–how do you feel you're doing in those three respective areas? Do you feel you keep the purpose of God first and foremost in your serving? How are you doing in working with different types of personalities?

## Historical Marker

*"There are two great days in a person's life—the day we are born and the day we discover why."*

–William Barclay

2. What happened when people focused on who Jesus was "after the flesh" instead of recognizing and respecting the office in which he stood? What kinds of problems can occur today if we know the pastor or another leader merely as a "buddy" or friend instead of recognizing the office in which he or she stands?

3. How do you think David could respect Saul as "the Lord's anointed" when he certainly wasn't acting like the Lord's anointed?

4. Do you agree with the statement that "every personality type has its strengths and weakness"? What are the strengths and weaknesses of your own personality? If there was a part of your personality that makes it difficult for others to work with you, what would it be, and what can you do to minimize the difficulty that area of your personality presents?

5. Have you ever allowed the carnality, immaturity, or a flaw in someone else's personality bring out the worst in you? Have you grown and made improvements in the area of not reacting to others?

6. Review the six traits of a Timothy that we covered in this lesson. How are you doing in those areas? Which trait do you feel you're strongest in? Which trait do you feel you need the most growth in?

7. Review the scriptures in the Fuel Stops. Which one speaks the most to you about where you are in your walk with and service toward God? Why?

8. Review the quotes in the Historical Markers. Which one is the most meaningful to you? Why?

9. What is one thing you learned from this lesson that you can apply to your life? How can it enhance the way you serve?

 **FUEL STOP**

**John 16:13**

13 However, when He, the Spirit of truth, has come, He will guide you into all truth; for He will not speak on His own authority, but whatever He hears He will speak; and He will tell you things to come.

# Off Road

## Proper Alignment: Your Car and Your Church

If you've driven a car for very long, you probably know what it's like to have one of your tires get out of alignment. Even though you've got four tires, if only one of them gets out of alignment, you've got a problem that needs to be addressed. What happens when a tire becomes misaligned?

- Misalignment can pull the car to the left or the right, in a different direction than what the driver intends. The steering wheel will not be centered when the car is moving straight ahead. There can be a feeling of looseness or wandering in the steering, as well as a vibration or shimmy in the steering.

- This becomes annoying to the driver who has to counter steer the car to keep it going straight and true.

## Historical Marker

*"A rock pile ceases to be a rock pile the moment a single man contemplates it, bearing within him the image of a cathedral."*

–Antoine de Saint-Exupery

- In addition to causing steering problems, misalignment can cause excessive and uneven tire wear, causing the tire to wear out sooner than it should. Worn tread can lead to a blow out.

- Because of the constant drag on the tire tread created by the misalignment, gasoline mileage will be negatively affected.

- Road shock can be increased, making the ride less smooth. The suspension can become overworked.

Experts tell us it's important to have a car's alignment checked periodically. This makes sense, as a properly aligned car can add thousands of miles to tire life, increase fuel economy, improve the handling of the car, make the ride more comfortable, and increase the overall safety of the vehicle.

## FUEL STOP

**1 Corinthians 16:10–11**

10 And if Timothy comes, see that he may be with you without fear; for he does the work of the Lord, as I also do.

11 Therefore let no one despise him. But send him on his journey in peace, that he may come to me; for I am waiting for him with the brethren.

What about being properly aligned in our church relationships? Just like one tire being out of alignment can cause problems for your car, one person—especially a leader or worker—who is "out of alignment" with others can pull in a different direction, cause premature "tire" wear, and create an uncomfortable ride for everyone.

Reread the above bullet points, and instead of thinking of your car, think of your church.

Great things happen when there is unity; great things can be hindered when there is misalignment. Many handling problems can be corrected by total alignment. With all the system components aligned properly, road shock is more efficiently absorbed for a smoother ride.

I believe that's why Paul said in 1 Corinthians 1:10 (NLT), *"I appeal to you, dear brothers and sisters, by the authority of our Lord Jesus Christ, to live in harmony with each other. Let there be no divisions in the church. Rather, be of one mind, united in thought and purpose."* The last part of that verse, in *The Message* version, reads, *"You must get along with each other. You must learn to be considerate of one another, cultivating a life in common."* Long before there were cars to illustrate the point, Scripture was already telling us of our need for proper alignment.

## Historical Marker

*"No member of a crew is praised for the rugged individuality of his rowing."*

—Ralph Waldo Emerson

## FUEL STOP

**Mark 6:2–6**

2 . . . He began to teach in the synagogue. And many hearing Him were astonished, saying, "Where did this Man get these things? And what wisdom is this which is given to Him, that such mighty works are performed by His hands!

3 Is this not the carpenter, the Son of Mary, and brother of James, Joses, Judas, and Simon? And are not His sisters here with us?" So they were offended at Him.

4 But Jesus said to them, "A prophet is not without honor except in his own country, among his own relatives, and in his own house."

5 Now He could do no mighty work there, except that He laid His hands on a few sick people and healed them.

6 And He marveled because of their unbelief.

## Travelogue

# Travelogue

# Lesson 6

## Packing for the Trip

🚗 In the textbook, *In Search of Timothy*, read

- Chapter 7, "Paul and Mark: If at First You Don't Succeed . . ."

- Chapter 8, "Paul and Others: Strategic Connections"

- Chapter 9, "Jesus and His Disciples"

🚗 Watch Lesson 6 on DVD

🚗 Work through this chapter in the workbook

## The Expressway

Not everyone will be a Timothy by title or position. In other words, not everyone can be *the* number two person in an organization, but everyone can be like Timothy in heart and attitude.

The final two traits of Timothy from Philippians 2:19–22 were discussed. God made each of us "deficient by design." He deliberately did not give any of us every gift, talent, and ability that is necessary. As such, we can never say that we don't need others, but instead, must work interdependently and in partnership to get the job done.

Timothy-Paul relationships are those where people are mutually respectful of each other's strengths and are not critical of each other's weaknesses. Instead, they use their mutual strengths to supplement and complement each other's ministry efforts.

There were others who helped Paul well at various times. He asked Timothy to bring Mark, saying that Mark was useful or profitable to him (2 Tim. 4:11). Mark, though, had not always been profitable to Paul. He had failed miserably on Paul's first missionary journey. If Mark could grow, mature, and develop, then each of us can also become profitable to the leader we work for.

## Historical Marker

*"What I do, you cannot do; but what you do, I cannot do. The needs are great, and none of us, including me, ever do great things. But we can all do small things, with great love, and together we can do something wonderful."*

—Mother Teresa

## FUEL STOP

**Romans 12:6**

6 Having then gifts differing according to the grace that is given to us, let us use them....

There were times when Paul had to stand alone in ministry, but he always preferred to work in partnerships with others as a team. Many brought great encouragement to Paul, such as Titus, Tychicus, Onesiphorus, and Priscilla and Aquila. A major focus of Jesus' ministry was to raise up individuals who would both follow Him and be able to fulfill leadership responsibilities.

## Of Titus . . .

*". . . a true son. . . ."* (Titus 1:4)

*". . . God, who comforts the downcast, comforted us by the coming of Titus"* (2 Cor. 7:6).

*"Titus . . . my partner and fellow worker. . ."* (2 Cor. 8:23).

*". . . Did we not walk in the same spirit? Did we not walk in the same steps?"* (2 Cor. 12:18).

## Of Tychicus . . .

*". . . a beloved brother, faithful minister, and fellow servant in the Lord . . . These are my . . . fellow workers for the kingdom of God . . . they have proved to be a comfort to me"* (Col. 4:7, 11).

## Of Onesiphorus . . .

*". . . he often refreshed me, and was not ashamed of my chain . . . he sought me out very zealously and found me . . . how many ways he ministered to me at Ephesus"* (2 Tim. 1:16–18).

## Of Priscilla and Aquila . . .

*". . . my fellow workers in Christ Jesus, who risked their own necks for my life, to whom . . . I give thanks . . ."* (Rom. 16:3–4).

## Of Stephanas, Fortunatus, and Achaicus . . .

*". . . what was lacking on your part they supplied. . . . They refreshed my spirit . . ."* (1 Cor. 16:17–18).

## Of Epaphroditus . . .

*". . . my brother, fellow worker, and fellow soldier . . . the one who ministered to my need"* (Phil. 2:25).

### Historical Marker

*"What is defeat? Nothing but education; nothing but the first step to something better."*

–Wendell Phillips

## Jesus' Strategy With His Disciples

Mark 3:13–15

13 And He went up on the mountain and called to Him those He Himself wanted. And they came to Him.
14 Then He appointed twelve, that they might be with Him and that He might send them out to preach,
15 and to have power to heal sicknesses and to cast out demons. . . .

# The Scenic Route

1. Can anyone be a Timothy? Not everybody in the church is going to be a Timothy by _____ or title, but everybody can become Timothy-like in spirit and in _____.

Refresher from last session: A Timothy is:

- Someone who inspires trust in the heart of a leader.

- Someone whose work in ministry encourages a spiritual leader.

- Someone who is accountable to the spiritual leader.

- Someone who is like-minded.

- Someone who sincerely cares.

- Someone who is not self seeking.

### FUEL STOP

**2 Timothy 4:11**
11 Get Mark and bring him with you, for he is useful to me for ministry.

"The definition of *steward* is 'one who manages the affairs of another.' "

"The church ultimately belongs to Jesus, and the gifts we've received originate from Him. Hence, when we serve in the church, we are stewards—we are managing the things that belong to God. How does this concept of stewardship relate to you in the light of these two verses?"

1 Corinthians 4:2 (Amplified)

2 . . . It is [essentially] required of *stewards* that a man should be found faithful [proving himself worthy of trust].

1 Peter 4:10

10 As each one has received a gift, minister it to one another, as good *stewards* of the manifold grace of God.

## The Final Two Characteristics of a Timothy

Philippians 2:19–22

19 But I trust in the Lord Jesus to send Timothy to you shortly, that I also may be encouraged when I know your state.

20 For I have no one like-minded, who will sincerely care for your state.

21 For all seek their own, not the things which are of Christ Jesus.

22 But you know his proven character, that as a son with his father he served with me in the gospel.

 **Historical Marker**

*"One compliment can keep me going for a whole month."*

—Mark Twain

2.  A Timothy is someone who has _____ character.

A person with *potential* is someone who could do it, but a person who is *proven* is someone who has done it. They have the experience and a proven track record of faithfulness and performance.

3.  A Timothy is someone who serves _____ a spiritual leader.

We can serve God in a number of ways. I'm not saying this is wrong, but there are some individuals who are serving God, but not with anyone else. Timothys are people who are serving *with* a spiritual leader; the way a son would serve with his father.

## FUEL STOP

**Acts 15:37–40**

37 Now Barnabas was determined to take with them John called Mark.

38 But Paul insisted that they should not take with them the one who had departed from them in Pamphylia, and had not gone with them to the work.

39 Then the contention became so sharp that they parted from one another. And so Barnabas took Mark and sailed to Cyprus;

40 but Paul chose Silas and departed. . . .

4. When we use the term, "deficient by design," we are indicating that God deliberately and intentionally did not give me and did not give you all of the _____ that exist. The Bible says that we have gifts differing according to the grace that is given to us (Rom. 12:6). There is only one individual who had all the gifts. Jesus had the Spirit without measure (John 3:34). The rest of us have a measure of the Spirit. We have certain gifts that are based on the grace that has been given to us and that's why we see different people with different abilities.

### Historical Marker

"*We deem it a sacred responsibility and genuine opportunity to be faithful stewards of all God has entrusted to us: our time, our talents, and our financial resources. We view all of life as a sacred trust to be used wisely.*"

–Moravian Covenant for Christian Living

5. God wisely chose to make us _____ upon one another. He wants us to recognize that we not only need divine help, but we need the partnership and the teamwork that comes from other people in the Body of Christ who have different gifts than what we have as well.

6. Timothy/Paul-type relationships are those where people are mutually _____ of each other's strengths and they are not _____ of each other's weaknesses. They use their mutual strengths to supplement and complement the ministries of each other.

## Mark

7. Paul requested that Timothy bring Mark with him because he believed that Mark would be _____ to him for the ministry.

> "Something struck me as a young assistant pastor. I realized that if Mark could be profitable to the spiritual leader that God had given him to work with, than perhaps I, too, could be profitable to the spiritual leader that God had assigned me to work with."

8. If we ever struggle with whether we are capable or adequate, it can help us to remember that Mark—the one who ultimately became profitable to Paul—had dismally _____ on his first missionary journey.

### FUEL STOP

**2 Timothy 4:11 (KJV)**

11 Take Mark, and bring him with thee: for he is profitable to me for the ministry.

9. From the story of Mark, we learn that people can be unprofitable at a certain point in their lives. We can be unprofitable because of a lack of maturity, commitment, or _____ problems. The good news is that we can grow up just as Mark did, and we can go from being unprofitable to being profitable. The traits of being profitable to a spiritual leader can be _____.

**Historical Marker**

*"Failure is the opportunity to begin again more intelligently."*

–Henry Ford

## Paul and Other Strategic Connections

10. At times, Paul had no choice but to work alone, but whenever he had the choice, he always preferred to work with a _____. He always preferred to work in _____ with others.

## Jesus and His Disciples

11. Jesus possessed a strong sense of urgency to raise up disciples who would be both _____ and _____.

12. Jesus chose people to work together, even though they would not, in the natural, have been _____.

13. Jesus' initial and top priority for the Twelve was not that they go out and preach, but that they were with Him. His top priority was _____, not missional. He wanted to have a relationship with them.

**FUEL STOP**

**Acts 13:13**
13 Now when Paul and his party set sail from Paphos, they came to Perga in Pamphylia; and John [Mark], departing from them, returned to Jerusalem.

14. Jesus had the twelve disciples _____ regularly.

   a) They provided transportation for Jesus. They rowed the boat while He slept.

   b) They arranged accommodations for Him when He traveled.

   c) Peter assisted in the paying of taxes.

   d) They helped in _____ matters. When Jesus miraculously multiplied the fish, He had His disciples seat the people in groups of fifty, distribute the food, and gather up the fragments.

   e) Jesus even had someone handling the ministry _____.

# Inspection Station

1.  When we consider the relatively low percentage of people who serve in their local churches, we are reminded of which of the following:

    a.  Many are not faithful stewards of the gifts, abilities, and talents that God has given them.

    b.  We–the church–are operating below our potential.

    c.  Metaphorically speaking, much of the Body of Christ is "paralyzed."

    d.  Much needs to be done to awaken believers to their calling so they can serve others, their pastor, and become vital contributors to the Body of Christ.

    e.  All of the above

2.  Which of the following statements is *not* true regarding Paul, Barnabas, and Mark?

    a.  Mark had not completed the first missionary journey with Paul and Barnabas, but returned to Jerusalem.

    b.  Paul wanted to give Mark a second chance, but Barnabas refused.

    c.  Mark ultimately became a fine minister even though he had an early failure.

    d.  Mark eventually wrote the Gospel of Mark.

    e.  In his last letter, Paul requested that Mark come and help him.

3.  Referring to a time when he was greatly discouraged (2 Cor. 7:6), Paul said that God had comforted him:

    a.  Through the appearance of an angel

    b.  By an audible voice

    c.  By the coming of Titus

    d.  Through a vision

    e.  None of the above

**FUEL STOP**

**Philippians 2:19–20**
But I trust in the Lord Jesus to send Timothy to you shortly, that I also may be encouraged when I know your state. For I have no one like-minded, who will sincerely care for your state.

4. In Second Timothy 1:16–18, Paul referred to a friend who had brought great encouragement into his life. He said that this friend had *". . . often refreshed me, and was not ashamed of my chain . . . he sought me out very zealously and found me . . . how many ways he ministered to me at Ephesus."* The name of this friend was:

   a. Stephanas

   b. Onesiphorus

   c. Tychichus

   d. Aquila

   e. Epaphroditus

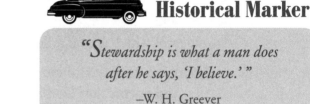

**Historical Marker**

*"Stewardship is what a man does after he says, 'I believe.'"*

—W. H. Greever

5. The one word that most accurately describes the majority of the people Jesus chose to serve Him is:

   a. Brilliant

   b. Orators

   c. Philosophers

   d. Achievers

   e. Ordinary

# Unpacking the Principles

1. In the teaching, Tony said, "Not everybody in the church is going to be a Timothy by position or title, but everybody can be Timothy-like in spirit and in heart." What does that statement mean to you, and what is the difference between position and attitude?

2. Rate yourself. How much are you like Timothy? Circle your response.

   • Do I inspire trust in the heart of my pastor? Yes / No

   • Do I encourage my pastor? Yes / No

   • Am I accountable to my pastor, or my supervisor? Yes / No

   • Am I like-minded with my pastor? Do I share the vision of the church? Yes / No

   • Do I sincerely care for others? Yes / No

- Have I moved beyond being self-seeking? Yes / No

- Have I proven myself? Have I done the work and produced solid results? Yes / No

- Do I serve with my pastor as a son serves with a father? Yes / No

For any of the above questions that you could not answer "yes," what can you do to strengthen that area of your service?

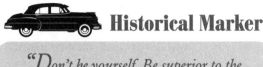

3. The word "like-minded" that Paul used to describe Timothy (Phil. 2:20) is from two Greek words meaning "equal soul." What does it mean for a follower to possess this trait in relationship to a spiritual leader? What does it not mean?

4. Paul sometimes used the human body as a metaphor to describe the church. (See Rom. 12:4–5 and 1 Cor. 12:12–27). What happens with a person when the different parts of his body don't function properly? What happens in the church when the different parts don't function properly?

5. What does it mean to realize that you (and others) are "deficient by design?" What should our attitudes and approach to working for God be in the light of that fact?

**FUEL STOP**

**1 Timothy 3:15**

15 . . . I write so that you may know how you ought to conduct yourself in the house of God, which is the church of the living God, the pillar and ground of the truth.

6. In the situation with Paul, Barnabas, and Mark, which of those three do you most relate to? Why? Have you ever had a relationship that was significantly strained, but then was restored into a healthy, working relationship?

7. In this lesson, we looked at several of Paul's relationships with people such as Titus, Tychicus, Onesiphorus, and so forth. Do you have friends like those who encourage you in your walk with God? Do you ever find yourself being an Onesiphorus or a Titus to others?

8. Most of the people Jesus chose are what we would call "ordinary" people. Why do you think Jesus did not search out only the most brilliant and accomplished people to be his disciples?

9. It was noted that some of Jesus' disciples, such as Matthew (a tax collector) would not have naturally been friends with Simon the Zealot. Why do you think that God sometimes calls people to work together for Him who might not otherwise be very socially compatible?

10. Have you ever known someone who seemed to have a good track record of working *for* God, but did not appear to have experienced much transformation in his or her character *from* God? What do you need to do to make sure that doesn't happen to you?

11. Review the scriptures in the Fuel Stops. Which one speaks the most to you about where you are in your walk with and service toward God? Why?

12. Review the quotes in the Historical Markers. Which one is the most meaningful to you? Why?

13. What is one thing you learned from this lesson that you can apply to your life? How can it enhance the way you serve?

## Historical Marker

*"The spirit of interdependence will not cost us more than it's worth. On the steep slope ahead, holding hands is necessary. And it just might be that we can learn to enjoy it."*

–Paul Harvey

## Off Road

### Lawrence Crabb's Story

In his book, *Encouragement: The Key to Caring* Larry Crabb shared that as a young boy, he had a serious problem with stuttering that caused him great embarrassment on many occasions. He further wrote:

"A short time later, our church celebrated the Lord's supper in a Sunday morning worship service. It was customary in our congregation to encourage young men to enter into the privilege of worship by standing and praying aloud. That particular Sunday I sensed the pressure of the saints (not, I fear, the leading of the Spirit), and I responded by unsteadily leaving my chair, for the first time, with the intention of praying.

"Filled less with worship than with nervousness, I found my theology becoming confused to the point of heresy. I remember thanking the Father for hanging on the cross and praising Christ for triumphantly bringing the Spirit up from the grave. Stuttering throughout, I finally thought of the word 'Amen' (perhaps the first evidence of the Spirit's leading), said it, and sat down. I recall staring at the floor, too embarrassed to look around, and solemnly vowing *never again* to pray or speak aloud in front of a group. Two strikes were enough.

## FUEL STOP

**John 3:34 (NLT)**
34 For he is sent by God. He speaks God's words, for God gives him the Spirit without limit.

"When the service was over, I darted toward the door, not wishing to encounter an elder who might feel obliged to correct my twisted theology. But I was not quick enough. An older Christian man named Jim Dunbar intercepted me, put his arm on my shoulder, and cleared his throat to speak.

"I remember thinking to myself, *Here it comes. Oh well, just endure it and then get to the car.* I then listened to this godly gentleman speak words that I can repeat verbatim today, more than twenty years later.

"'Larry,' he said, 'there's one thing I want you to know. Whatever you do for the Lord, I'm behind you one thousand percent.' Then he walked away.

**Historical Marker**

"*Stewardship is the act of organizing your life so that God can spend you.*"

–Lynn A. Miller

"Even as I write these words, my eyes fill with tears. I have yet to tell that story to an audience without at least mildly choking. Those words were *life* words. They had power. They reached deep within my being. My resolve never again to speak publicly weakened instantly.

"Since the day those words were spoken, God has led me into a ministry in which I regularly address and pray before crowds of all sizes. I do it without stuttering. I love it. Not only death, but also life, lies in the power of the tongue."[1]

## Travelogue

_____

_____

_____

_____

_____

_____

_____

_____

_____

_____

_____

# Travelogue

# Lesson 7

## Packing for the Trip

🚗 In the textbook, *In Search of Timothy*, read

- Chapter 10, "John the Baptist: Promoting the Success of Another"
- Chapter 11, "Moses and Those Who Helped Him"

🚗 Watch Lesson 7 on DVD

🚗 Work through this chapter in the workbook

 ## The Expressway

The team Jesus assembled didn't just listen and learn; they worked! They carried out a number of practical assignments that helped Jesus and the rest of the team. They arranged transportation and lodging, set up meals, and so forth. They took care of details so Jesus could focus on his primary assignment.

When the apostles delegated the responsibility of daily food distribution to the seven faithful men in Acts 6, they were likely implementing the practice of delegating what they had learned from Jesus. Sometimes the disciples misrepresented Jesus, and He had to train them so they would know His heart and represent Him properly.

John the Baptist showed an attitude of deferring to Jesus when John said, "He must increase, and I must decrease" (John 3:30). He was willing to take a secondary role and focus on helping Jesus to be successful.

## Historical Marker

> "*If this world is going to be reached, I am convinced that it must be done by men and women of average talent.*"
>
> –Dwight L. Moody

Moses relied on individuals such as Joshua and Aaron to work in teamwork and partnership with him. Jethro–Moses' father-in-law–taught Moses the importance of delegating and letting others share the load. Moses initially put people into positions of leadership, but it was later that these individuals received the same Spirit that the Lord had placed on Moses. God wants His leaders to be surrounded by anointed, like-minded team members.

# The Scenic Route

1. Jesus picked very _____ people, and yet because of their association with Him, they became very extraordinary people.

2. Jesus' disciples often took care of natural details so Jesus could focus on His primary _____.

3. Jesus had disciples that made _____.

   a) James and John wanted to call down _____ from heaven to destroy a certain village of people.

   b) The disciples wanted to send away a woman who was seeking healing for her daughter, but Jesus went ahead and healed the woman's daughter.

   c) The disciples wanted to send a multitude away but Jesus wanted to _____ that multitude.

   d) The disciples rebuked those who brought _____ to Jesus so He would bless them. But Jesus said, "Don't hinder them, let the children come to me" (Luke 18:16).

## FUEL STOP

**Ephesians 4:11–12**

11 And He Himself gave some to be apostles, some prophets, some evangelists, and some pastors and teachers,

12 for the equipping of the saints for the work of ministry, for the edifying of the body of Christ. . . .

4. Jesus had disciples who _____ Him. Jesus had to correct and train them so they would know His heart and represent Him properly.

> "John the Baptist's attitude was not, 'How successful can I be?' or 'How popular can I be?' His attitude was, 'How successful and popular can I help Jesus become?' "

### Historical Marker

> "*The world is full of willing people; some willing to work, the rest willing to let them.*"
> —Robert Frost

5. When Moses was feeling inadequate about the assignment God was giving him, perhaps the most reassuring thing God told him was, *"I will certainly be _____ you"* (Exod. 3:12).

6. In the story of Joshua leading the Israelite army against the Amalekites, one of the lessons we learn is that _____ had a part to play.

   a) Moses' part represented _____ and intercession.

   b) Aaron and Hur had the responsibility of supporting Moses by holding up his _____ until the sun went down.

   c) Joshua had a responsibility to _____ the army, and the army had the responsibility to _____ the battle.

7. What we see in this and countless other stories in the Word of God is that when everybody does their part the job gets _____. When everybody does their part, then we see _____.

8. Before Jethro gave Moses counsel (Exod. 18), Moses' leadership style could be summed up as Moses trying to do everything by _____.

> "When Jethro saw Moses trying to meet all of the needs of the people himself, he said to Moses, 'This is not good! You're going to wear yourself out—and the people, too. This job is too heavy a burden for you to handle all by yourself' " (Exod. 18:17–18).

### FUEL STOP

**Mark 10:13–14**

13 Then they brought little children to Him, that He might touch them; but the disciples rebuked those who brought them.

14 But when Jesus saw it, He was greatly displeased and said to them, "Let the little children come to Me, and do not forbid them; for of such is the kingdom of God."

9. The counsel that Jethro gave Moses consisted of:

   a) **Pray**: (Exod. 18:19) "_____ before God for the people, so that you may bring the difficulties to God."

   b) **Teach, Show, and Delegate**: (Exod. 18:20) "*You shall teach them the statutes and the laws, and show them the way in which they must walk and the _____ they must do.*"

   c) **Appoint**: (Exod. 18:21) "*You shall _____ from all the people able men, such as fear God, men of truth, hating covetousness; and place such over them to be rulers of thousands, rulers of hundreds, rulers of fifties, and rulers of tens.*"

   d) **Release and Supervise**: (Exod. 18:22) "*And _____ them judge the people at all times. Then it will be that every great matter they shall bring to you, but every small matter they themselves shall judge. So it will be easier for you. . . .*"

10. Unfortunately, when it comes to the work of the ministry, many church people have the mistaken notion that the _____ is supposed to do it all. The Bible teaches that the ministry gifts that Jesus has given—and this includes pastors—are responsible to _____ the saints so that the saints can do the work of the ministry (Eph. 4:11–12).

11. In Numbers 11, Moses was still struggling under the stress and feeling alone in carrying the burden and the responsibility of the people. The pressure was so great that he even expressed a desire to _____ (Num. 11:15).

12. It's not enough for those who are assigned to help leaders to simply have _____ and job descriptions. God's solution was to take of the _____ that was upon Moses and place the same upon his helpers (Num. 11:17).

## FUEL STOP

**Exodus 17:9–13**

9 And Moses said to Joshua, "Choose us some men and go out, fight with Amalek. Tomorrow I will stand on the top of the hill with the rod of God in my hand."

10 So Joshua did as Moses said to him, and fought with Amalek. And Moses, Aaron, and Hur went up to the top of the hill.

11 And so it was, when Moses held up his hand, that Israel prevailed; and when he let down his hand, Amalek prevailed.

12 But Moses' hands became heavy; so they took a stone and put it under him, and he sat on it. And Aaron and Hur supported his hands, one on one side, and the other on the other side; and his hands were steady until the going down of the sun.

13 So Joshua defeated Amalek and his people with the edge of the sword.

> "When God put the Spirit that was upon Moses upon all the others leaders, it wasn't to reduce Moses' role as the leader in any way. Moses was still called to be the leader. He was still the one that God dealt with and God gave instructions to. But God knew that Moses couldn't do it alone, and that he couldn't do it unless the people on the team were on the same page spiritually. They had to be under the same anointing."

13. Perhaps saying that the elders had "the same Spirit" upon them that Moses had is a somewhat similar concept to what Paul said when he referred to Timothy as being like-_____.

14. When it came to the Tabernacle, God gave Moses the plans—or the _____. Moses then passed on the plans to workers whom God had anointed to do the actual work. God wants His leaders to be surrounded by anointed, like-minded team members.

 **Historical Marker**

*"Opportunity is missed by most people because it is dressed in overalls and looks like work."*

–Thomas Edison

 **Inspection Station**

1. Which of the following statements is *not* true about John the Baptist?

   a. John the Baptist clearly understood that he was not in competition with Jesus.

   b. John the Baptist was not territorial about his position. He was not concerned about having less popularity or attention than Jesus had.

   c. Referring to Jesus, John the Baptist said, "He must decrease, but I must increase."

   d. John understood that "we" is more important than "me."

   e. None of the above is false. They are all true statements.

 **FUEL STOP**

**Acts 6:1–4**

1 Now in those days, when the number of the disciples was multiplying, there arose a complaint against the Hebrews by the Hellenists, because their widows were neglected in the daily distribution.

2 Then the twelve summoned the multitude of the disciples and said, "It is not desirable that we should leave the word of God and serve tables.

3 Therefore, brethren, seek out from among you seven men of good reputation, full of the Holy Spirit and wisdom, whom we may appoint over this business;

4 but we will give ourselves continually to prayer and to the ministry of the word."

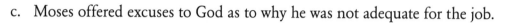

2. Which of the following statements are true about Moses when he was called by God?

a. He had been out in the wilderness for 40 years and probably didn't feel he was at his peak performance level.

b. He probably felt as though his purpose had been aborted when he killed the Egyptian and fled Egypt and that God had no further use for him.

c. Moses offered excuses to God as to why he was not adequate for the job.

d. God assured Moses that He would be with him, and said that Aaron, his brother, would assist him as well.

e. All of the above

3. Which of the following statements is *not* true regarding the situation where God took the Spirit that was upon Moses and placed the same Spirit on all the other leaders (Num. 11:14–17)?

**FUEL STOP**

**Exodus 18:19–23**

19 Listen now to my voice; I will give you counsel, and God will be with you: Stand before God for the people, so that you may bring the difficulties to God.

20 And you shall teach them the statutes and the laws, and show them the way in which they must walk and the work they must do.

21 Moreover you shall select from all the people able men, such as fear God, men of truth, hating covetousness; and place such over them to be rulers of thousands, rulers of hundreds, rulers of fifties, and rulers of tens.

22 And let them judge the people at all times. Then it will be that every great matter they shall bring to you, but every small matter they themselves shall judge. So it will be easier for you, for they will bear the burden with you.

23 If you do this thing, and God so commands you, then you will be able to endure, and all this people will also go to their place in peace.

a. Moses had been at a breaking point and had begun to see the people as a burden.

b. When God placed the same Spirit on Moses' leaders, it made all of them (including Moses) coequal in leadership.

c. God's plan was for these seventy to bear the burden of the people with Moses.

d. God's plan was for all of the leaders to be operating under the same anointing of the Holy Spirit.

e. None of the above is false. They are all true statements.

# Unpacking the Principles

1. It was noted that Jesus' helpers took care of natural details so that Jesus could focus on His primary assignment. It was also noted that in the Early Church (Acts 6), the apostles allowed others to take care of certain assignments so they could give themselves to prayer and the ministry of the Word. How important do you feel this pattern is in the church today? How well is this biblical example being implemented?

**Historical Marker**

*"It is only as we develop others that we permanently succeed."*

—Harvey S. Firestone

2. Several instances were referred to when Jesus' disciples misrepresented Him. Looking back over your Christian life and service, have you ever misrepresented Jesus' attitude or love to others? Are any adjustments needed in your life in this area?

3. Can you relate in any way to the story that Tony told about the drummer? Would you be willing to relinquish a role you enjoyed and serve in another area if doing so would benefit the church?

4. Can you relate to the inadequacy Moses expressed when God called him to ministry? Have you ever felt that you were incapable of doing something that God was asking you to do and realized that without His enablement, you couldn't do it? What were your excuses? How did that situation work out?

5. In Exodus 17, we saw how Moses' hands were held up and steadied by Aaron and Hur. Have you ever found yourself in a role where you felt you were giving the same kind of support and assistance to a leader? Do you see your role in your church reflecting that same attitude of support?

6. In the video, Tony said, "We need to cast not only our cares on the Lord, but we also need to cast other people's cares on the Lord. We are not called to carry—in an emotionally unhealthy sense—everybody's burdens." How are you doing in this regard? Do you tend to carry other peoples' burdens, and if so, what can you do to begin to change that?

**FUEL STOP**

**Exodus 39:42–43**

42 According to all that the Lord had commanded Moses, so the children of Israel did all the work.

43 Then Moses looked over all the work, and indeed they had done it; as the Lord had commanded, just so they had done it. And Moses blessed them.

7. When it came to delegation, "let them" may have been the hardest words Moses ever heard (Exod. 18:22). Do you ever have trouble delegating responsibility to others—even when others are available? And if so, why?

## FUEL STOP

**Matthew 15:23**

23 His disciples came and urged Him, saying, "Send her away, for she cries out after us."

8. Tony presented two different philosophies about pastors and the work of the ministry. The first one he presented is the idea that, "We pay our pastor so he can do all the work." The second mentality is that "We pay our pastor so he can get us to do the work." What do you think of those two approaches?

9. Have you ever known someone who was a hard worker *until* they were given a title or a position, and afterwards were less reliable, enthusiastic, or productive? Whether we have a title or a position, or not, what should our focus always be regarding our role in kingdom work?

10. Review the scriptures in the Fuel Stops. Which one speaks the most to you about where you are in your walk with and service toward God? Why?

11. Review the quotes in the Historical Markers. Which one is the most meaningful to you? Why?

12. What is one thing you learned from this lesson that you can apply to your life? How can it enhance the way you serve?

## Historical Marker

*"It is the men behind who make the man ahead."*

–Merle Crowell

## Off Road

Xvxn though this typxrwritxr is an old modxl, it works wxll xxcxpt for onx kxy. It is trux that thxrx arx 41 kxys that function wxll xnough, but just onx kxy not working makxs thx diffxrxncx.

Somxtimxs it sxxms that an organization is somxwhat likx this typxrwritxr, not all thx kxys arx working propxrly.

You may say to yoursxlf, "Wxll, I am only onx pxrson. I won't makx or brakx a program." But it doxs makx a diffxrxnce bxcausx any program, to bx xfficixnt, nxxds thx activx participation of xvxry mxmbxr.

So thx nxxt timx you think you arx only onx pxrson and that your xfforts arx not nxxdxd, rxmxmbxr this typxwritxr and say to yoursxlf, "I am a valuablx pxrson."

–Unknown

## Historical Marker

*"The difference between something good and something great is attention to detail."*

–Charles Swindoll

When looking at that typewriter, all of the keys might look equally fine. The problem is that one of them doesn't put the letter on the page. It's not an issue of how the key looks; it's about function and results. It's not about appearance; it's a matter of getting the letters on the page.

Consider how one employee in a hotel made a huge difference in the life of one of their customers:

A room service waiter at a Marriott hotel learned that the sister of a guest had just died. The waiter, named Charles, bought a sympathy card, had hotel staff members sign it and gave it to the distraught guest along with a piece of hot apple pie.

The guest later wrote this letter to the president of Marriott Hotels:

> *"Mr. Marriott, I'll never meet you. And I don't need to meet you because I met Charles. I know what you stand for. . . . I want to assure you that as long as I live, I will stay at your hotels and tell my friends to stay at your hotels."*[1]

Charles certainly represented Mr. Marriott and the entire hotel chain well, but what happens when a worker in a church doesn't function the way he or she is supposed to? The finished product ends up looking far different than what it could or should. Just like Moses couldn't do all that needed to be done without the contributions of many others, neither can any pastor today.

I'm convinced that our rewards in heaven are not going to be based on what titles or positions we held, but on what was actually produced from God's grace at work in our lives. Remember the lesson of the old typewriter and remember the story of Charles, and say to yourself, "I am a valuable person. I can make a significant contribution."

 **FUEL STOP**

**Numbers 11:14–17**

14 "I am not able to bear all these people alone, because the burden is too heavy for me.

15 If You treat me like this, please kill me here and now—if I have found favor in Your sight—and do not let me see my wretchedness!"

16 So the Lord said to Moses: "Gather to Me seventy men of the elders of Israel, whom you know to be the elders of the people and officers over them; bring them to the tabernacle of meeting, that they may stand there with you.

17 Then I will come down and talk with you there. I will take of the Spirit that is upon you and will put the same upon them; and they shall bear the burden of the people with you, that you may not bear it yourself alone."

# Travelogue

# Lesson 8

## Packing for the Trip

🚗 In the textbook, *In Search of Timothy*, read

- Chapter 12, "David and Jonathan: Knitted Souls"

- Chapter 13, "David and His Brave Warriors"

- Chapter 14, "Elisha: An Example of True Follower-ship"

🚗 Watch Lesson 8 on DVD

🚗 Work through this chapter in the workbook

 **The Expressway**

Great things don't happen just because one person decides they should. It takes many people working together to create the finished product. Paul, Jesus, and Moses all had help, and so did David.

One of the great supporters and helpers in David's life was his friend Jonathan. Jonathan was not only loyal, but his heart was knit to the heart of David. And that was the basis of their covenant. Unfortunately, most of the love we see today is "convenient" love, not "covenant" love.

In addition to Jonathan, David was supported by his "Mighty Men." David was looking for individuals who came in peace, who came to help, and with whom his heart could be united. There is a difference between the congregation and the core, and David set high standards for his core team.

Amasai led the core group in pledging themselves to David in loyalty. They weren't worshipping David, but they were recognizing God's call upon David's life and committing themselves to work in partnership with him. David and his men showed great honor and respect toward each other. Elijah was also greatly helped in his ministry through the partnership of Elisha.

## Historical Marker

> "*Great souls are always loyally submissive, reverent to what is over them: only small, mean souls are otherwise.*
>
> –Thomas Carlyle

# The Scenic Route

1. Great things don't happen because one person _____ they should. It takes many people working together to create the finished product.

2. There are two types of love in the earth today. The first kind of love and the rarest kind of love is _____ love, where individuals make a quality commitment to love, honor, respect, protect, and serve each other regardless of the cost.

3. The far more common type of love in the earth today is what we might call _____ love. This type of love says, "I'll help you if it's easy—if I don't have other things to do and if it fits my schedule.

## FUEL STOP

**1 Samuel 18:1, 3–4**

1 . . . the soul of Jonathan was knit to the soul of David, and Jonathan loved him as his own soul.

3 Then Jonathan and David made a covenant, because he loved him as his own soul.

4 And Jonathan took off the robe that was on him and gave it to David, with his armor, even to his sword and his bow and his belt.

4. Even though Jonathan was the legal heir to the throne, he believed it was his assignment in life to _____ and help David be successful and become the next king. Jonathan had to have the same kind of attitude regarding David that _____ the _____ had concerning Jesus, which was: "He must increase, but I must decrease."

5. If it had not been for _____, there would have never been a David. He served in such a way so that David was protected, preserved, and promoted.

6. Jonathan didn't put David on a pedestal to _____ him. He simply recognized the level of high _____ and high calling that was upon David's life. Jonathan was committed to doing whatever he could to help David step into and fulfill the calling that David had received from the Lord.

### Historical Marker

> "*A religion that gives nothing, costs nothing, and suffers nothing, is worth nothing.*"
>
> –Martin Luther

7. David didn't always have a lot of people helping and supporting him, but there came a point in his life and ministry when the call of God upon his life became evident, and people began coming to him (1 Chron. 12:18–22). When they did, David made it clear that he was looking for people who:

   a) Came in _____, because he knew he didn't need troublemakers.

   b) Came to _____, because he knew he didn't need spectators.

   c) Could be _____ with him, because he knew he didn't need people who would be promoting their own, personal agendas.

### FUEL STOP

**2 Kings 3:11**

11 But Jehoshaphat said, "Is there no prophet of the Lord here, that we may inquire of the Lord by him?" So one of the servants of the king of Israel answered and said, "Elisha the son of Shaphat is here, who poured water on the hands of Elijah."

8. The reason David laid out such strong expectations is because he wasn't simply looking to build a _____; he was looking to build a _____.

9. Jesus not only ministered to the multitudes, or "congregation," but He also had a core. The closer in, or the higher up, that people were in the core, the more that was _____ of them.

"As a leader, David was looking for people who genuinely sensed and believed that they were not in his life by accident. He was looking for people that God had ordained to cross his path so that strategic alliances and connections could be established. He was looking for God-birthed, God-ordained, and God-blessed relationships. In short, he was looking for what we call divine connections."

10. Divine connections are what:

   a) _____ referred to when he spoke of Timothy being "like-minded."

   b) The Old Testament elders had when they received the same _____ that Moses had.

   c) _____ and Jonathan experienced when their souls were knit together.

### Historical Marker

*"There is one element that is worth its weight in gold and that is loyalty. It will cover a multitude of weaknesses."*

–Philip D. Armour

11. After David issued his challenge, Amasai, the spokesman for the 30 men, said, *" 'We are _____, O David! We are with you, O son of Jesse! Success, success to you, and success to those who _____ you, for your God will help you' "* (1 Chron. 12:18 NIV).

"The word translated *success* in First Chronicles 12:18 (NIV) is the Hebrew word *shalom*. It refers to completeness, wholeness, and soundness in every dimension of one's being: spiritually, emotionally, socially, physically, and financially."

12. When David was in the cave and expressed a desire for some water from Bethlehem, three of his mighty men _____ through the Philistine lines and brought the water to him. Instead of drinking the water, David poured it out as a drink _____ to the Lord (1 Chron. 11:15–19). This was not a sign of disrespect from David. Rather, it was the highest honor he could have given these men. In essence, he was saying, "Your act of service, devotion, courage, and consecration is so sacred that I cannot take this water and indulge myself with it. I have to give it to God as an act of _____; it's too holy for me to consume upon myself."

## FUEL STOP

**1 Samuel 14:6–7 (NLT)**

6 "Let's go across to the outpost of those pagans," Jonathan said to his armor bearer. "Perhaps the Lord will help us, for nothing can hinder the Lord. He can win a battle whether he has many warriors or only a few!"

7 "Do what you think is best," the armor bearer replied. "I'm with you completely, whatever you decide."

"David and his men built a bond of trust and honor. God wants us to have such honor in our relationships that we are willing to go to extravagant lengths to serve one another. When that service is given and rendered, it can be given and rendered mutually to one another. David's men showed him the highest honor and respect, and David showed that same honor and respect back to them."

13. _____ became a servant to Elijah. After Elijah's departure, the king asked if there was a prophet in the land. Elisha was then referred to as the one who had poured _____ on the hands of Elijah. Elisha was not referred to here as a great prophet or as one who had great revelation. He was known as one who had _____ another prophet.

# Inspection Station

1. What phrase is used to describe the connection between Jonathan and David in First Samuel 18:1?

   a. Jonathan was like-minded to David.

   b. Jonathan had the same spirit on him that David had.

   c. The soul of Jonathan was knit to the soul of David.

   d. A three-fold cord is not easily broken.

   e. All of the above

2. In First Samuel 14:7 (NLT) we read the statement, *"'Do what you think is best. . . . I'm with you completely, whatever you decide.'"* Who made that statement, and to whom was it made?

   a. David's armor bearer to David

   b. Jonathan's armor bearer to Jonathan

   c. David to King Saul

   d. Jonathan to King Saul

   e. David's brother, Eliab, to David

## Historical Marker

*"Far too often in a church staff environment, we incorrectly apply grace. Someone makes a mistake or falls short of a standard of excellence and we say, 'Ah, that's okay.' It's not okay. Jesus didn't die on the Cross for 'okay.' He deserves our best. You can be kind in your communication and patient in your coaching, but don't lower your expectations. The cause of Christ is worth everyone's best."*

—Dan Reiland

3. In First Chronicles 12:16–17, when David was in the cave and a group of men came to him, David responded by:

   a.  Immediately enlisting them to be a part of his team

   b.  Communicating expectations about the motives and attitudes he expected if they were to unite with him

   c.  Rejecting them and sending them back to their homes

   d.  Evaluating very carefully their talents and skills

   e.  Both A and D

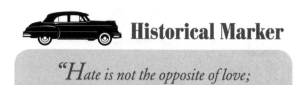

### Historical Marker

*"Hate is not the opposite of love; apathy is."*

–Rollo May

4. Which of the following statements is true of Jesus?

   a.  He ministered to the multitudes.

   b.  He had a group of 70 that He helped develop and train.

   c.  He had a group of 12 that were even closer to Him than the 70.

   d.  Within that group of 12, he had an inner circle of three who were closer yet.

   e.  All of the above

### FUEL STOP

**Matthew 5:9**

9 Blessed are the peacemakers, For they shall be called sons of God.

# Unpacking the Principles

1.  Do you feel like you've seen and experienced in life both "covenant love" and "convenient love?" What have you seen to be the fruit of these two types of love?

2.  What is the difference between a congregation and a core? Why are there different levels of expectations, and what types of different expectations might be reasonably applied to each of the two groups?

3.  How did the core/congregation issue apply to Jesus and those who followed Him? With whom did he spend most of his time? What did He expect from the different groups, and why were those expectations different?

4. When we speak of "divine purpose," do you feel like you are just randomly bouncing through life, or do you believe that you are truly engaging in Kingdom work that is God-ordained and of eternal significance? How would a person know the difference between the two?

5. Tony spoke of a situation where there could be "external compliance while there is still internal rebellion." How do you think that could happen with a believer?

6. Amasai said to David, *"'We are yours, O David! We are with you, O son of Jesse!'"* (1 Chron. 12:18 NIV). What is the difference between loyal support and putting the leader on a pedestal?

7. What did you think of the mutual respect and devotion between David and his three mighty men in the matter of the water from the well in Bethlehem? Does such a story have relevance today? If so, how?

8. Review the scriptures in the Fuel Stops. Which one speaks the most to you about where you are in your walk with and service toward God? Why?

9. Review the quotes in the Historical Markers. Which one is the most meaningful to you? Why?

10. What is one thing you learned from this lesson that you can apply to your life? How can it enhance the way you serve?

## Historical Marker

*"There's a difference between interest and commitment. When you are interested in doing something, you do it only when it is convenient. When you are committed to something, you accept no excuses."*

—Ken Blanchard

## Off Road

Isaiah 41:6–7

6 Everyone helped his neighbor,
And said to his brother,
"Be of good courage!"
7 So the craftsman encouraged the goldsmith;
He who smooths with the hammer inspired him who strikes the anvil,
Saying, "It is ready for the soldering";
Then he fastened it with pegs,
That it might not totter.

## FUEL STOP

**1 Chronicles 11:15–19**

15 Now three of the thirty chief men went down to the rock to David, into the cave of Adullam; and the army of the Philistines encamped in the Valley of Rephaim.

16 David was then in the stronghold, and the garrison of the Philistines was then in Bethlehem.

17 And David said with longing, "Oh, that someone would give me a drink of water from the well of Bethlehem, which is by the gate!"

18 So the three broke through the camp of the Philistines, drew water from the well of Bethlehem that was by the gate, and took it and brought it to David. Nevertheless David would not drink it, but poured it out to the Lord.

19 And he said, "Far be it from me, O my God, that I should do this! Shall I drink the blood of these men who have put their lives in jeopardy? For at the risk of their lives they brought it." Therefore he would not drink it. These things were done by the three mighty men.

The first time I read these verses in Isaiah, I was excited about the great teamwork demonstrated by all of these laborers. It was obvious to me that they were in unity, and they were excited about what they were building. They had a great sense of camaraderie, and they were literally cheering each other on during the building process. They were committed to quality. They did not want what they were building to totter or wobble. They wanted it to be strong, stable, and lasting. I was excited because there was no sense of competition among the workers, but they seemed to truly value and respect the various contributions of each of the other laborers. You can almost see them giving each other "high fives" as each one completed their particular aspect of the work.

## Historical Marker

*"He is no fool who gives what he cannot keep to gain what he cannot lose."*

—Jim Elliot

As I was enjoying their great unity and teamwork, I realized that I didn't know what they were building. Surely this must have been a truly wonderful and magnificent project for them to give of themselves in such a way. I decided to check some commentaries, and was shocked to see that these men who were so unified were building *idols*—false gods. I was so disappointed. I thought these verses would have made such a great example, but in my mind, *what* they were building messed everything up. Then I realized, *Wait a minute. If they can be that unified and enthusiastic about building something that is completely worthless, how much more should we—the children and servants of the Most High God—be about doing the work He has called us to do in building the Kingdom of God upon the earth!*

May our teamwork, unity, camaraderie, and sense of purpose always be energized by the One for whom we work as we fulfill His cause upon the earth!

## FUEL STOP

**1 Chronicles 12:16–18, 21–22 (NIV)**

16 Other Benjamites and some men from Judah also came to David in his stronghold.

17 David went out to meet them and said to them, "If you have come to me in peace, to help me, I am ready to have you unite with me. But if you have come to betray me to my enemies when my hands are free from violence, may the God of our fathers see it and judge you."

18 Then the Spirit came upon Amasai, chief of the Thirty, and he said: "We are yours, O David! We are with you, O son of Jesse! Success, success to you, and success to those who help you, for your God will help you." So David received them and made them leaders of his raiding bands.

21 They helped David against raiding bands, for all of them were brave warriors, and they were commanders in his army.

22 Day after day men came to help David, until he had a great army, like the army of God.

# Travelogue

# Travelogue

# Lesson 9

## Packing for the Trip

🚗 In the textbook, *In Search of Timothy*, read

- The introduction to Part III, "The Traits of Great Supportive Ministers"
- Chapter 15, "Great Supportive Ministers Are Loyal"
- Chapter 16, "Great Supportive Ministers Have Excellent Attitudes"

🚗 Watch Lesson 9 on DVD

🚗 Work through this chapter in the workbook

## The Expressway

This session addresses the traits and characteristics that typify a great servant like Timothy. A survey among several pastors revealed that loyalty was the most highly desired trait among top leaders and workers in churches. Unfortunately, some individuals appear to be loyal, but inwardly are rebellious and critical. Ruth, Ittai, and Joab were cited as Old Testament examples of loyalty.

Tony shared an experience from when he was young in ministry where, as an assistant pastor, someone complimented him and at the same time criticized the pastor. Tony realized that it would be wrong to try to make himself look good at the pastor's expense, and he spoke positively about the pastor to that person. Tony realized he was there to represent the pastor and to be an extension of his ministry.

Having the right attitude is another essential characteristic of being a great supportive minister, even more important than talent and ability. When we have attitude problems, our tendency is to blame our bad attitude on some other person or on some circumstance. While we don't have the ability to choose every circumstance we face in life, we always have the choice about what our attitude is going to be, and we need to choose to maintain a good attitude in life.

Faithfulness is also essential for supportive ministers, and the Lord expects us to be faithful, even in things that we consider small. Some people think only of ability, but God wants us to offer Him our availability. Faithfulness involves giving God the best of our time and energy, being reliable, punctual, consistent, dependable, and paying attention to details.

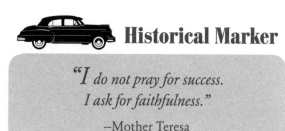

**Historical Marker**

*"I do not pray for success. I ask for faithfulness."*

–Mother Teresa

# The Scenic Route

1. It is important to identify the _____ and characteristics of someone who is like Timothy.

2. **Trait #1:** Pastors who responded to a survey indicated that _____ was the most desired and admired trait among church leaders and workers.

## FUEL STOP

**Romans 14:17–19 (NLT)**

17 For the Kingdom of God is not a matter of what we eat or drink, but of living a life of goodness and peace and joy in the Holy Spirit.

18 If you serve Christ with this attitude, you will please God, and others will approve of you, too.

19 So then, let us aim for harmony in the church and try to build each other up.

3. Individuals can develop an outward appearance of loyalty but internally be grumbling, complaining, and developing attitudes of _____ and disloyalty.

4. _____ is a character in the Bible who exhibited strong loyalty when she said to Naomi, "*'Don't urge me to leave you or turn back from you. Where you go I will go, and where you stay I will stay. Your people will be my people and your God my God. Where you die I will die, and there I will be buried. . . .'*" (Ruth 1:16–17 NIV).

### Historical Marker

"*A*bility is what you're capable of doing. Motivation determines what you do. Attitude determines how well you do it."

–Lou Holtz

5. Another example of loyalty is when Ittai said to King _____, "*As surely as the Lord lives, and as my lord the king lives, wherever my lord the king may be, whether it means life or death, there will your servant be'*" (2 Sam. 15:21 NIV).

6. _____ was one of David's military leaders who exhibited loyalty when he said, "*. . . gather the rest of the people together and encamp against the city and take it, lest I take the city and it be called after my name*" (2 Sam. 12:28)

## FUEL STOP

**Matthew 6:33**
33 But seek first the kingdom of God and His righteousness, and all these things shall be added to you.

"A loyal person is not out to advance or promote himself. He's really out to help the team be successful, and he's happy to give credit to others."

7. When Tony visited people in the hospital as an assistant pastor, he understood that he was doing that as an _____ of the senior pastor. He was his pastor's _____.

"Don't allow anyone to drive a wedge of competition between you and the pastor, or you and any other team member. This is not a popularity contest. This is not a talent contest. This isn't about who can be the most liked. This is a matter of a team working together to carry out ministry."

8. **Trait #2:** Great supportive ministers have an excellent _____.

9. Attitude beats _____. You can train people in the area of skills, but attitude has to come from within. Attitude is one of the greatest _____, one of the greatest components that you could ever bring into a leadership and serving relationship.

10. Tony said, "I made up my mind very early on that I did not want to become one of the _____ that the pastor had to deal with. I didn't want my attitude to become a burden to him in any way shape or form. I wanted to contribute to my pastor's praise life, not to inspire his prayer life. I wanted to lift him up, not drag him down. I wanted to make his job easier, not harder. I wanted to be a _____ maintenance, _____ output individual.

### Historical Marker

"*I don't know what your destiny will be, but one thing I know: the only ones among you who will be really happy are those who have sought and found a way to serve.*"

—Albert Schweitzer

11. If you focus on flaws, faults, shortcomings, and imperfections, you're going to remain agitated and _____. But we need to have the attitude that says, "God I'm going to look for the _____ in things, and I'm going to bring the best out of every situation that I can."

12. **Trait #3:** Great supportive ministers are _____.

### FUEL STOP

**Matthew 5:41**

41 And whoever compels you to go one mile, go with him two.

13. It seems to be a human tendency to think that when God gives us some great big assignment, *then* we're going to be tremendously faithful. But God doesn't operate on that system. God wants to see if we are going to be faithful in the seemingly _____ things.

14. So many times we focus on ability, but God wants to know if there is _____. You can't even begin to be faithful to something unless you've made yourself available to it.

15. What are the traits of a faithful person?

   a) Careful to fulfill a promise, _____; you can believe them. When they say they're going to do something, they're going do it.

   b) Dedicated in carrying out duties and responsibilities.

   c) Diligent in work.

   d) Dependable in completing assignments. You can count on their work being done.

e) Thorough; not just a good _____, but also a great finisher; doesn't "drop the ball" halfway through the project.

f) Pays attention to details; doesn't let things "fall through the cracks."

g) _____; shows up on time and meets deadlines.

h) Consistent and constant; not up one day and down the next.

i) Doesn't just look good on the surface, but is solid through and through.

j) _____ and trustworthy; isn't underhanded or sneaky.

k) Meets and exceeds expectations; doesn't just do enough to get by but is willing to go the extra mile.

16. Pastors are looking for faithful people–people they can _____ on, people that are dependable, people they can _____.

17. In spite of facing great betrayal and rejection in life, _____ is a great biblical example of faithfulness.

 **Inspection Station**

1. The idea of loyalty can include:

   a. A commitment to a relationship and to the welfare of that person

   b. Being unswerving in allegiance

   c. Being faithful to a person to whom fidelity is due

   d. Being faithful to a cause or an idea

   e. All of the above

 **FUEL STOP**

**Matthew 25:21**

21 His lord said to him, "Well done, good and faithful servant; you were faithful over a few things, I will make you ruler over many things. Enter into the joy of your lord."

2. Which of the following statements is *not* true of our work in the church?

   a. When we receive an assignment, we should see ourselves as a representative of the pastor, not as his replacement.

   b. We should see ourselves as a part of the overall team, not as a "solo act."

   c. It's okay if people compliment us while criticizing the senior pastor.

   d. We should never exploit a situation to make ourselves look good at the pastor's expense.

   e. None of the above is false. They are all true statements.

**FUEL STOP**

**Song of Solomon 2:15**
15 Catch us the foxes, the little foxes that spoil the vines. . . .

3. Which of the following statements is *not* true concerning our attitude?

   a. Our attitude is just one of many situations in life that we have no control over.

   b. When people have a bad attitude, they often tend to blame that bad attitude on another person or circumstance.

   c. In any given situation, we can choose to focus on the positive or the negative.

   d. No one else can make you have a bad attitude without your cooperation.

   e. None of the above is false. They are all true statements.

**Historical Marker**

"*Loyalty to the pastor does not mean blindly following and agreeing with everything he or she does. It means as long as the pastor is giving biblical leadership, as a leader, you are to support your pastor even if you might do things different yourself.*"

–Dan Reiland

4. A bad attitude will undermine which of the following:

   a. A great calling and anointing

   b. Talent and ability

   c. Experience and education

   d. Overall effectiveness

   e. All of the above

# Unpacking the Principles

1.  What were your reflections as you considered the material on loyalty? Have you personally seen some great examples of loyalty? Have you seen examples of disloyalty? What positive and negative effect did you see these examples have on the team?

2.  Tony mentioned an example of when a person tried to drive a wedge between him and the pastor he was serving. Have you ever experienced the same, and if so, how did you respond?

### Historical Marker

*"Two men looked through prison bars; one saw mud, the other saw stars."*

–Unknown

3.  What did you think of the concept about an assistant, in the course of his work, seeing his job as "representing the pastor" as opposed to "replacing the pastor?"

4.  What are your thoughts on the attitude versus ability issue? Have you ever observed someone who seemed to have great ability but a poor attitude? What effect did that seem to have on the team?

5.  Have you ever found yourself focusing on the flaws and faults in a situation to the point where you lost your ability to see and appreciate the good that was there? What did you do to bring yourself out of that faultfinding perspective?

6.  As you went over the list of the traits of a faithful person, which areas did you believe to be your strongest? Were there areas that you saw where you could use improvement?

7.  Review the scriptures in the Fuel Stops. Which one speaks the most to you about where you are in your walk with and service toward God? Why?

### FUEL STOP

**Ruth 1:16–17**

16 But Ruth said: "Entreat me not to leave you, Or to turn back from following after you; For wherever you go, I will go; And wherever you lodge, I will lodge; Your people shall be my people, And your God, my God.
17 Where you die, I will die, And there will I be buried. The Lord do so to me, and more also, If anything but death parts you and me."

8.  Review the quotes in the Historical Markers. Which one is the most meaningful to you? Why?

9.  What is one thing you learned from this lesson that you can apply to your life? How can it enhance the way you serve?

## Off Road

### Keeping Rank

1 Chronicles 12:33 (KJV)

33 Of Zebulun, such as went forth to battle, expert in war, with all instruments of war, fifty thousand, which could *keep rank:* they were not of double heart.

### Historical Marker

*"A great attitude is not the result of success; success is the result of a great attitude."*

–Earl Nightingale

The ability to keep rank, to stay in one's place, and to serve faithfully is a great attribute. No doubt that these highly disciplined men of Zebulun were greatly appreciated and valued by David.

As we serve, there are two things we can do: we can *keep rank* or we can *break rank.*

To *keep rank* means that we stay focused on our assignment, and we do not deviate from our purpose, calling, or assigned duties.

There is a great scene in the movie *Gladiator* where Maximus and his fellow gladiators have been thrust into the coliseum to fight a seemingly insurmountable enemy. They are on foot in the middle of the arena. Multiple chariots with horses and better equipped warriors are about to come charging in to attack them. At that point, Maximus says to his men, *"Whatever comes out of these gates, we've got a better chance of survival if we stick together. Do you understand? If we stay together, we survive."* When the attack begins, the men who ignore Maximus' plea and allow themselves to be isolated are picked off easily. However, those who stay together and fight together, do, in fact, survive and actually triumph.

In church, we understand that we may serve in certain areas for a season and then move on to something else, but we should never "break rank" in a rebellious way that hurts others. Jude verse 6 referred to *"the angels who did not keep their proper domain, but left their own abode. . . ."* That's certainly an example we don't want to follow.

Sometimes, we may find it necessary to "keep rank" even if some around us do not do the same. One of the Old Testament heroes of faith and one of David's mighty men was an individual named Shammah. He did exactly that; he kept rank when others abandoned their posts. Consider the following:

### FUEL STOP

**2 Chronicles 19:9**

9 And he commanded them, saying, "Thus you shall act in the fear of the Lord, faithfully and with a loyal heart."

## Historical Marker

*"Nothing can stop the man with the right mental attitude from achieving his goal; nothing on earth can help the man with the wrong mental attitude."*

–W.W. Ziege

2 Samuel 23:11–12

11 And after him was Shammah the son of Agee the Hararite. The Philistines had gathered together into a troop where there was a piece of ground full of lentils. So the people fled from the Philistines.

12 But he stationed himself in the middle of the field, defended it, and killed the Philistines. So the Lord brought about a great victory.

Shammah kept rank and defended a bean patch, and God called it a great victory! Even though others abandoned their post, neglected their assignment, and were not faithful, Shammah was. What a great blessing you will be to the Kingdom of God, to your church, and to your pastor when you keep rank! What's even better is when everyone on the team keeps rank, but make sure you keep rank whether others do or not!

## FUEL STOP

**2 Samuel 15:19–21**

19 Then the king said to Ittai the Gittite, "Why are you also going with us? Return and remain with the king. For you are a foreigner and also an exile from your own place.

20 In fact, you came only yesterday. Should I make you wander up and down with us today, since I go I know not where? Return, and take your brethren back. Mercy and truth be with you."

21 But Ittai answered the king and said, "As the Lord lives, and as my lord the king lives, surely in whatever place my lord the king shall be, whether in death or life, even there also your servant will be."

## Travelogue

_____

_____

_____

_____

_____

_____

# Travelogue

# Lesson 10

## Packing for the Trip

🚐 In the textbook, *In Search of Timothy*, read

- Chapter 17, "Great Supportive Ministers Are Faithful"

- The first part of Chapter 18, "Great Supportive Ministers 'Play Well With Others'" through and including the section "Submission: Relating Well to the Pastor"

🚐 Watch Lesson 10 on DVD

🚐 Work through this chapter in the workbook

 ## The Expressway

Joseph is an amazing example of faithfulness. Even when life gave him the very worst, he continued to give his best. In spite of great setbacks, Joseph served diligently. Whether he was a slave in Potiphar's house or a prisoner who had been falsely accused, Joseph served with such excellence that he ended up running the house and the prison, and ultimately served as Prime Minister of Egypt.

Tony shared the story of Bob who was a man who came to the Lord from a rough background. God, however, put a servant's heart inside of Bob. He ended up serving his pastor and church in a most exemplary way. This was a blessing to the pastor, because he had previously felt as though he had to do so many things himself.

But Bob didn't just serve when he was asked to do so. He was proactive in looking for opportunities and avenues through which he could be a blessing. Because God put "helps" (1 Cor. 12:28) in his heart, Bob began to be more thoughtful and considerate of others, even though he didn't have an official title or position. He simply began to look for ways to serve and help others, especially the pastor.

Borrowing from our elementary school report cards, it was pointed out that another trait of great supportive ministers is the ability to "play well with others." To relate to those who serve in positions of authority, we need to have an attitude of submission.

 **Historical Marker**

> "*The ultimate measure of a man is not where he stands in moments of comfort and convenience, but where he stands at times of challenge and controversy.*"
>
> —Martin Luther King Jr.

 **The Scenic Route**

1. Trait #3 continued: _____

2. Genesis 39:2 tells us that the Lord was with Joseph and blessed him greatly as he _____.

3. Joseph had every reason to have a bad _____, to wallow in self-pity, to feel that life had not been fair, to feel that he wasn't appreciated. He had been rejected, and yet he chose to serve with all of his heart and give his very best. And the Lord blessed him because of that servant's heart.

4. Joseph's attitude was, "If I'm going to be a slave, then I'm going to be the _____ slave in Egypt. If I'm going to be a prisoner, then I'm going to be the _____ prisoner in the entire prison."

**FUEL STOP**

**1 Corinthians 12:28**

28 And God has appointed these in the church: first apostles, second prophets, third teachers, after that miracles, then gifts of healings, helps, administrations, varieties of tongues.

5. Because Joseph attended so faithfully to administrative details, he was a great blessing to those who were his overseers or supervisors. Joseph released his supervisors from _____ clutter and from the menial duties. Joseph took care of all those matters because of his faithfulness.

**Historical Marker**

"*Do not pray for easy lives.
Pray to be stronger men.
Do not pray for tasks equal to your powers.
Pray for powers equal to your tasks.*"

–Phillips Brooks

6. There are many people who want to receive blessing, but not as many people who are positioning themselves to be a _____.

7. In First Corinthians 12:27–28, there is a list of gifts that God has set in the church. That list includes apostles, prophets, teachers, miracles, gifts of healings, _____, administrations, and varieties of tongues.

**FUEL STOP**

**Genesis 39:21–23 (NLT)**

21 But the Lord was with Joseph in the prison and showed him his faithful love. And the Lord made Joseph a favorite with the prison warden.

22 Before long, the warden put Joseph in charge of all the other prisoners and over everything that happened in the prison.

23 The warden had no more worries, because Joseph took care of everything. The Lord was with him and caused everything he did to succeed.

8. When a "helps mentality" begins to manifest in a person, he or she will typically become less _____ centered and become more courteous, kind, and thoughtful toward others.

9. If we are unreliable in our duties and responsibilities, then things are going to be left undone. The church will not _____ at the proper level of effectiveness and excellence.

**Trait #4:** Great supportive ministers "play well with others."

10. "Playing well with others" is seen on three different dimensions:

a) Getting along with those in _____, or those who are above us.

b) Getting along with our coworkers, those who are on an equal plane.

c) Getting along with those who are under our supervision, people who we may direct or _____ their work.

11. The key word to getting along well with those in authority is _____.

> *"Submission is not a popular word in our society, because many people don't want to be submitted to anyone or anything. Perhaps they've had bad experiences with authority situations that were unhealthy or they may have been in some kind of situation that worked to their detriment. So they're leery and reluctant to trust anyone. Yet the fact remains that submission is a biblical concept."*

12. According to Hebrews 13:17, the _____ or _____ that is experienced by a pastor is going to be largely dependant on how submissive and cooperative the people are.

13. Any of the following types of people can make the pastor's job a grievous experience.

   a) Rebellious

   b) Full of strife and division

   c) Second-guessing everything

   d) _____

   e) Hard-hearted and stiff-necked

   f) Projecting the "I'm not going to volunteer; I'm not going to give" attitude

**Historical Marker**

*"When you forgive someone, you set a prisoner free . . . and then you find that the prisoner was you."*

–Lewis Smedes

14. On the other hand, the following types of attitudes can truly make the pastor's job a _____.

   a) "Pastor, you're providing spiritual leadership. We're going to obey the Word of God."

   b) "We're going to serve one another."

   c) "We're going to cooperate."

   d) "We're going to bring our tithes and offerings."

   e) "We're going to _____."

   f) "We're going to love."

   g) "We're going to pray."

**FUEL STOP**

**Hebrews 13:17**

17 Obey those who rule over you, and be submissive, for they watch out for your souls, as those who must give account. Let them do so with joy and not with grief, for that would be unprofitable for you.

# Inspection Station

1.  In Acts 6, the Apostles declined to "serve tables" because:

    a.  They felt it was beneath their dignity.

    b.  They didn't think there was a legitimate need.

    c.  They believed they needed to keep their focus on prayer and the ministry of the Word.

    d.  They thought it was better to simply preach against complaining.

    e.  None of the above

2.  In order to function in the ministry of helps, a person must:

    a.  Be a Bible school graduate

    b.  Be a gifted preacher and/or teacher

    c.  Have a high-ranking position or title within the church

    d.  Be willing to serve

    e.  Work directly under the senior pastor's supervision

3.  The phrase, "plays well with others," has to do with what issues?

    a.  Our people skills

    b.  The way we interact with others

    c.  Getting along harmoniously with others

    d.  Bringing out the best in others

    e.  All of the above

## Historical Marker

"*A diamond is a chunk of coal that made good under pressure.*"

–Unknown

## FUEL STOP

**Genesis 39:2–6 (NLT)**

2 The Lord was with Joseph, so he succeeded in everything he did as he served in the home of his Egyptian master.

3 Potiphar noticed this and realized that the Lord was with Joseph, giving him success in everything he did.

4 This pleased Potiphar, so he soon made Joseph his personal attendant. He put him in charge of his entire household and everything he owned.

5 From the day Joseph was put in charge of his master's household and property, the Lord began to bless Potiphar's household for Joseph's sake. All his household affairs ran smoothly, and his crops and livestock flourished.

6 So Potiphar gave Joseph complete administrative responsibility over everything he owned. With Joseph there, he didn't worry about a thing—except what kind of food to eat!

# Unpacking the Principles

1. Can you identify with Joseph? Have you ever been trying to do the right thing only to encounter setbacks? Did you find it easy to persevere in serving God, or were you tempted to wallow in self-pity or become resentful?

2. Do you feel like you tend to only do what is asked of you, or can you relate to Bob, who "was proactive in looking for opportunities and avenues through which he could be a blessing."

**Proverbs 25:19 (NLT)**
19 Putting confidence in an unreliable person in times of trouble is like chewing with a broken tooth or walking on a lame foot.

3. Do you feel that "helps" is just as important as the other gifts mentioned in First Corinthians 12:27–28 (apostles, prophets, teachers, miracles, etc.)? Why or why not?

4. Are you the kind of church member that you would want to have in the church if you were the pastor? What traits do you feel you possess and exhibit that would make your pastor's job a joy? Do you possess or exhibit any traits that might make your pastor's job grievous? If so, what adjustments might you need to make?

5. Review the scriptures in the Fuel Stops. Which one speaks the most to you about where you are in your walk with and service toward God? Why?

6. Review the quotes in the Historical Markers. Which one is the most meaningful to you? Why?

7. What is one thing you learned from this lesson that you can apply to your life? How can it enhance the way you serve?

## Historical Marker

"*Nothing in the world can take the place of persistence. Talent will not; nothing is more common than unsuccessful men with talent. Genius will not; unrewarded genius is almost a proverb. Education will not; the world is full of educated derelicts. Persistence and determination alone are omnipotent. The slogan 'Press On' has solved and always will solve the problems of the human race.*"

–Calvin Coolidge

# Off Road

There was some discussion in this lesson, based on Hebrews 13:17, about the need for church members to be submissive and obedient. That verse indicates this will help your pastor's job be joyful and not grievous. Below are some things you can do for your pastor:

1. Pray Fervently: Pray for your pastor and the pastor's spouse and family.

2. Respect Sincerely: Be respectful and courteous. Honor your pastor as a gift from God. Esteem him highly in love for his work's sake.

## Historical Marker

*"He who cannot obey, cannot command."*

—Benjamin Franklin

3. Give Generously: Support your church financially. Bring your tithes and offerings into the storehouse.

4. Serve Joyfully: Serve in the church. Give freely of your time to the ministries and the programs of your church.

5. Compensate Appropriately: Do all you can do to make sure your pastor is properly compensated. First Timothy 5:17–18 says, *"Let the elders who rule well be counted worthy of double honor, especially those who labor in the word and doctrine. For the Scripture says, 'You shall not muzzle an ox while it treads out the grain,' and, 'The laborer is worthy of his wages.'"* In addition to a good salary and compensation package, bless your pastor on special occasions such as birthdays, anniversaries, and Christmas. Receive a special offering so the pastor's family can go on a nice vacation. Don't be like the stingy people who prayed, "God, you keep our pastor humble, and we'll keep him poor."

6. Refresh Frequently: Make sure your pastor is able to attend continuing education events each year just for ministers. The pastor's skills need to be refreshed and sharpened, and he needs to be ministered to also. If your church does not have it in the budget for the pastor to attend some of these events, a special offering is in order. The cost of the pastor's continuing education and spiritual refreshing is something that the church cannot afford not to do. It is one of the best financial investments the church can make.

7. Expect Reasonably: We all have certain expectations of spiritual leaders, but some expectations can be unfair and impossible to meet. Pastors are human beings. They are not perfect, nor do they have perfect spouses or children. Many pastors' children have been hardened to church, and the things of God because of harsh, judgmental attitudes coming from church members.

## FUEL STOP

**1 Peter 2:17**

17 Honor all people. Love the brotherhood. Fear God. Honor the king.

# Travelogue

<h1 style="text-align:right">Lesson 11</h1>

## Packing for the Trip

🚗 In the textbook, *In Search of Timothy*, read

- Chapter 18, "Great Supportive Ministers 'Play Well With Others' " beginning with "Teamwork: Relating Well to Other Leaders and to Coworkers"

- Chapter 19, "Great Supportive Ministers Have a Servant's Heart"

- Chapter 20, "Great Supportive Ministers Are Energetic and Enthusiastic"

- Chapter 21, "Great Supportive Ministers Are Balanced"

🚗 Watch Lesson 11 on DVD

🚗 Work through this chapter in the workbook

## The Expressway

"Playing well with others" has three dimensions: 1) relating well to those in authority; 2) relating well to our peers and coworkers; and 3) relating well to those we supervise. To do this, we must exercise submission, teamwork, and diplomacy, respectively.

When we are part of a support team in church, it's important that we are not in competition with each other. We are called to complete each other, not to compete against each other. It

## Historical Marker

doesn't matter how skilled, talented, or anointed we might be if we can't walk in love—being submitted to those in authority, walking in teamwork with our coworkers, and treating those under our supervision with kindness.

Great supportive ministers also have a servant's heart. Jesus not only taught this, He embodied this principle with His life. Great supportive ministers are also energetic and enthusiastic. It's okay to come to church to get energized and motivated. But it's better to come to church and share that enthusiasm with others. No leader likes to pull dead weight or try to motivate people who are not excited or interested in getting things done for the Kingdom of God.

In addition to being fervent, supportive ministers also need to be balanced. This involves having a proper emphasis of worship, work, rest, and play in our lives. We need to balance work and family, tasks and relationships, the natural and the supernatural, and seriousness and humor.

## The Scenic Route

1. How well we relate to other people is a huge part of our effectiveness serving in the church because we can't serve people well if we're always in _____, misunderstandings, or division with people.

2. The key word to getting along with our coworkers is the word _____.

3. When we are part of a support team in church work, it's very important that we not be in _____ with others around us. Instead, we need to respect and encourage their ministries.

**FUEL STOP**

**John 20:21**
21 "As the Father has sent Me, I also send you."

4. A critical question that we must ask: Are we competing against each other or are we _____ each other?

5. The third level of "playing well with others" has to do with relating well with those under our _____. The key word here is_____.

> "It doesn't matter how skilled, talented, or anointed we might be. If we can't walk in love with one another, if we can't be submitted to those in leadership, if we can't cooperate in teamwork with those who are our coworkers, if we can't treat those who are under our supervision with kindness, then it really makes no difference how much ability we have. Our ability doesn't matter if we can't play well with others."

### Historical Marker

> "*Be kind, for everyone you meet is fighting a hard battle.*"
> —Plato

6. **Trait #5:** Great supportive ministers have a _____ heart.

7. Jesus not only taught this, but He _____ and embodied it.

> "Ministry is not about titles and position; it is not about recognition and prestige; it is about serving others with the love of God and with the gifts and abilities that God has given us."

8. **Trait #6:** Great supportive ministers are energetic and _____.

> "*Enthusiasm* comes from the Greek word *entheos*. *En* means "in, or within;" and *theos* means "god." *Entheos* means "having the god within." It was first used in English in 1603 and meant, "possession by a god."

9. There's nothing wrong with coming to church to get built up and energized, but it's even better to get built up and *then* come to church. It's okay to come to church to get motivated, but it's even better to get _____ and then bring that motivation to church.

10. No leader likes to pull _____ weight or try to motivate people who are not excited and interested in getting things done for the Kingdom of God.

### FUEL STOP

**Ecclesiastes 9:10**

10 Whatever your hand finds to do, do it with your might. . . .

> "We need churches today that are full of fire, excited, energetic, and wanting to make a difference in the world. Pastors want supportive ministers who exhibit passion, zeal, eagerness, and enthusiasm in their work for the Lord. They want people who are industrious and willing to bring energy into their work."

11. **Trait #7:** Great supportive ministers are _____ people.

12. There are times that we need to _____ as well as to work.

13. The four areas that Richard Exley said we need to have balanced in our lives are:

    a) _____

    b) Work

    c) _____

    d) Play

14. We also need proper balance in the area of _____ and relationships. Some people need to work at improving their relationship skills; other people need to work at improving their task accomplishment skills.

15. It's been said that some people are so heavenly minded, they're no earthly good and others are so _____ minded, they're no heavenly good. We need balance, between the natural and the _____.

16. We need balance between seriousness and _____. We need to take our calling very seriously but not ourselves so seriously.

## Inspection Station

1. Which of the following statements is *not* true when it comes to servanthood?

    a. When it comes to church and the work of the church, we should be willing to do whatever it takes to get the job done.

**FUEL STOP**

**Colossians 1:29 (NIV)**
29 To this end I labor, struggling with all his energy, which so powerfully works in me

b. Jesus did not come to serve, but to be served.

c. The people who are the greatest asset in the local church are those who do not feel they are "too good" to do certain things.

d. Jesus demonstrated servanthood when He washed the feet of the disciples.

e. None of the above is false. They are all true statements.

## Historical Marker

*"I expect to pass through life but once. If, therefore, there can be any kindness I can show, or any good thing I can do to any fellow being, let me do it now and not defer or neglect it, as I shall not pass this way again."*

–William Penn

2. Which of the following statements is true when it comes to the type of energy God's people are to invest in working for the Kingdom?

a. Whatever your hand finds to do, do it with your might.

b. Not lagging in diligence, fervent in spirit, serving the Lord.

c. Never be lazy, but work hard and serve the Lord enthusiastically.

d. Never lag in zeal and in earnest endeavor; be aglow and burning with the Spirit, serving the Lord.

e. All of the above

3. Those who rebuilt the walls of Jerusalem were said to have "had a mind to work," or according to another translation, "the people worked with all their heart." Under whose leadership were these people working?

a. Hezekiah

b. Ezra

c. Nehemiah

d. Bezalel

e. Josiah

## FUEL STOP

**1 Corinthians 13:4–5, 7** (Amplified)

4 Love endures long and is patient and kind; love never is envious nor boils over with jealousy, is not boastful or vainglorious, does not display itself haughtily.

5 It is not conceited (arrogant and inflated with pride); it is not rude (unmannerly) and does not act unbecomingly. Love (God's love in us) does not insist on its own rights or its own way, for it is not self-seeking; it is not touchy or fretful or resentful; it takes no account of the evil done to it [it pays no attention to a suffered wrong].

7 Love bears up under anything and everything that comes, is ever ready to believe the best of every person, its hopes are fadeless under all circumstances, and it endures everything [without weakening].

4. According to Philippians 2:29–30, which New Testament figure came close to dying because he didn't take care of himself?

    a.  Epaphroditus

    b.  Apollos

    c.  Titus

    d.  Tychicus

    e.  Onesimus

### Historical Marker

*"There's no limit to what we can accomplish if no one cares who gets the credit."*

—Ronald Reagan

# Unpacking the Principles

1. How are you doing in the area of "Plays Well With Others?"

   • Toward those in authority? Are you submissive and cooperative?

   • Toward your coworkers? Are you a good team player?

   • Toward those you supervise? Are you kind and encouraging?

2. Jesus perfectly personified what it means to have a servant's heart when He washed the feet of the disciples. What are some ways we can effectively demonstrate having that kind of heart toward each other today?

3. Have you ever told God, "God, I'll serve you in any way, except _____?" Do you believe that you've truly surrendered your life to serve God in any way He would ask?

4. Reread First Corinthians 13:4–5, 7 (Amplified) from page 101. How well do you personify and exemplify the traits of love as described in those verses?

5. Who is someone that brings energy and enthusiasm to the team? What effect does it have? How much energy and enthusiasm do *you* bring to the team?

6. How are you doing in the following areas of balance?

   • Worship, Work, Rest, and Play?

   • Work and Family?

   • Tasks and Relationships?

   • The Natural and the Supernatural?

   • Seriousness and Humor?

   What are some practical steps you can take to improve concerning the areas that need improvement?

### FUEL STOP

**Romans 12:11** (Message)

11 Don't burn out; keep yourselves fueled and aflame. Be alert servants of the Master. . . .

7. Review the scriptures in the Fuel Stops. Which one speaks the most to you about where you are in your walk with and service toward God? Why?

8. Review the quotes in the Historical Markers. Which one is the most meaningful to you? Why?

 **Historical Marker**

> "*History has been written not by the most talented, but by the most motivated.*"
>
> —Peter Drucker

9. What is one thing you learned from this lesson that you can apply to your life? How can it enhance the way you serve?

 **Off Road**

A simple and basic definition of Christianity might read something like this: "Christianity is a relationship between God and man through Jesus Christ." While I agree that this statement is correct, I don't think it's a complete or comprehensive description. Why? Because this definition only addresses the *vertical* aspect of God's plan for our life and entirely omits the *horizontal* commands of Christianity. It's entirely true that our relationship with God is a vital part of what Christianity is all about, but the Bible continuously stresses the need to fulfill our responsibilities toward one another. Consider the following list of "one another" Scriptures:

 **FUEL STOP**

**Matthew 20:25–28**

25 But Jesus called them to Himself and said, "You know that the rulers of the Gentiles lord it over them, and those who are great exercise authority over them.

26 Yet it shall not be so among you; but whoever desires to become great among you, let him be your servant.

27 And whoever desires to be first among you, let him be your slave—

28 just as the Son of Man did not come to be served, but to serve, and to give His life a ransom for many."

- Love one another (John 13:34)

- Be kindly affectionate to one another with brotherly love (Rom. 12:10)

- In honor prefer one another (Rom. 12:10)

- Live in harmony with one another (Rom. 12:16 NIV)

- Pursue the things which make for peace and the building up of one another (Rom. 14:19)

- Receive one another (Rom. 15:7)

- Admonish one another (Rom. 15:14)

- Serve one another (Gal. 5:13)

- Bear one another's burdens (Gal. 6:2)

- Be kind and tenderhearted to one another (Eph. 4:32)

- Forgive one another even as God for Christ's sake has forgiven you (Eph. 4:32)

- Teach and admonish one another (Col. 3:16)

- Increase and abound in love toward one another (1 Thess. 3:12)

- Comfort one another (1 Thess. 4:18)

- Edify one another (1 Thess. 5:11)

- Exhort one another (Heb. 3:13)

- Confess your faults one to another and pray one for another, that you may be healed (James 5:16 Amplified)

- Be hospitable to one another (1 Peter 4:9)

- Love one another (1 & 2 John, multiple references)

The Apostle John made it clear that "loving God" and "loving people" are inseparable propositions. Further, he made it clear that a "theoretical love" or giving mental assent to the idea of love is not what God was referring to.

### Historical Marker

*"There are people with a lot more talent than I have who have been weeded out of the league because they couldn't put their egos aside to fill a role."*

—Kurt Rambis

**FUEL STOP**

**John 13:14–15**

14 If I then, your Lord and Teacher, have washed your feet, you also ought to wash one another's feet.

15 For I have given you an example, that you should do as I have done to you.

1 John 4:20–21 (Message)

20 If anyone boasts, "I love God," and goes right on hating his brother or sister, thinking nothing of it, he is a liar. If he won't love the person he can see, how can he love the God he can't see?
21 The command we have from Christ is blunt: Loving God includes loving people. You've got to love both.

1 John 3:18 (Amplified)

18 Little children, let us not love [merely] in theory or in speech but in deed and in truth (in practice and in sincerity).

Love must be practiced, and I can't think of any higher expression of the love of God than service. This happens when we obey the "one anothers" of Scripture.

# Travelogue

# Travelogue

# Lesson 12

## Packing for the Trip

🚗 In the textbook, *In Search of Timothy*, read

- Chapter 22, "Great Supportive Ministers Are Flexible and Growth-Oriented"

- Chapter 23, "Great Supportive Ministers Are Internally Motivated"

- Chapter 24, "Great Supportive Ministers Are Good Communicators"

- Chapter 25, "Great Supportive Ministers Multiply Themselves"

- Chapter 26, "Great Supportive Ministers Are People of Integrity and Honesty"

- Chapter 27, "Great Supportive Ministers Exercise Wisdom in Their Pulpit Ministry"

- Chapter 28, "Great Supportive Ministers Exercise Discretion"

🚗 Watch Lesson 12 on DVD

🚗 Work through this chapter in the workbook

## The Expressway

Great supportive ministers are flexible and growth-oriented. Some things, such as the Gospel and the Word of God, do not change and should not change. Other things, such as styles and methods, can and should be changed at times to maintain freshness and relevance to a changing society. We need wisdom to know the difference between the negotiable and the nonnegotiable. We also need sensitivity and honesty to know what needs to change in our own lives for us to be the best servants we can possibly be.

Great supportive ministers are also internally motivated. There is something burning within their hearts to please God and to serve others. Part of being internally motivated involves knowing when to take initiative. Another trait of great supportive ministers is that they are good communicators, and this begins with being a good listener and observer. Communication also involves providing reports and feedback to the appropriate people and through the proper channels.

Great supportive ministers also multiply themselves. It's great to be a good worker, but it's even better if you can inspire, recruit, train, supervise, and ultimately release others to be workers as well. Great supportive ministers are also people of integrity and honesty. They keep their word, and if they make a mistake, they admit it. They're not blame shifters and excuse makers.

In addition, great supportive ministers exercise wisdom in their pulpit ministry. They respect those areas of communication that belong to the senior pastor and leave those areas alone. Finally, great supportive ministers exercise discretion. This involves having the wisdom to say and do the right things at the right time and avoiding things that are inappropriate and in poor taste. Maintaining confidentiality is also an important part of discretion.

 **Historical Marker**

*"Integrity is one of several paths. It distinguishes itself from the others because it is the right path, and the only one upon which you will never get lost."*

–M.H. McKee

 **The Scenic Route**

1. **Trait #8:** Great supportive ministers are _____ and growth-oriented.

 **FUEL STOP**

**Malachi 3:16** (Amplified)
16 Then those who feared the Lord talked often one to another. . . .

2. The words of a _____ church are, "We've never done it that way before." We've got to know where to change, adapt, and be flexible. Yet at the same time, we need to know where to be enduring, solid, and consistent on the nonnegotiable areas of the Word of God.

3. What are of the traits of flexible, growth-oriented people?

   a) They are life-long _____.

   b) They're willing to address and overcome weaknesses in their life.

c) They're open to new _____ and new ways of doing things.

d) They adjust graciously to unexpected developments.

e) They adapt to other people.

f) They are willing to embrace new assignments or relinquish old roles for the good of the church.

g) They continually seek _____.

h) They experience spiritual vitality in their lives.

## Historical Marker

*"Even if you're on the right track, you'll get run over if you just sit there."*

–Will Rogers

**Trait #9:** Great supportive ministers are internally motivated.

4. What's even better than someone else giving you a goal from the outside is when you have a higher goal for quality and excellence on the _____ of you.

5. There are three types of people in life: those who _____ things happen, those who watch things happen, and those who aren't sure what happened.

6. In addition to taking initiative, we also have to be what is called amenable. To be amenable means that we are submitted and that we are accountable to and we _____ for what we do. We want to take initiative, but we also need to have the wisdom to know when we need to get _____ before we take initiative.

**Trait #10:** Great supportive ministers are great communicators.

7. The first step in being a great communicator is to be a good _____.

8. Supportive ministers need to provide the proper _____ to the proper people through the proper channels.

9. **Trait #11:** Great supportive ministers _____ themselves.

## FUEL STOP

**Psalm 110:3**
3 Your people shall be volunteers in the day of Your power. . . .

10. It's one thing to do ministry, it's another thing to _____ ministers.

11. Great supportive ministers have learned the art of inspiring and _____ others to help in the work.

12. **Trait #12:** Great supportive ministers are people of _____ and honesty.

13. What are some of the traits of people who have integrity and honesty in their lives?

   a) They are aboveboard, honorable, and _____ in all of their dealings.

   b) They are not deceitful. They don't do things in secret that they would be ashamed of in the light.

   c) They tell the _____. If they are wrong and make a mistake, they admit it–they accept responsibility for their actions.

   d) They don't shift blame, spin, slant, or twist the story to their own advantage.

   e) They don't say things that are technically true in one sense, but actually give a false _____ of the overall situation.

   f) They are accurate in stating the facts. They don't embellish or exaggerate the facts, and they don't withhold pertinent and appropriate information.

   g) They keep their word; they do what they say they're going to do. They don't make rash, impulsive _____ that they can't or don't intend to keep.

   h) They say "yes" when they mean yes and they say "no" when they mean no.

14. God wants us to be honest, virtuous, and have integrity in our dealings with one another. When honesty, virtue, and integrity exist in a church culture, and they exist among leaders, workers, and volunteers, then the basis for _____ is created.

**FUEL STOP**

**Proverbs 11:3**
3 The integrity of the upright will guide them, But the perversity of the unfaithful will destroy them.

15. **Trait #13:** Great supportive ministers exercise wisdom in their _____ ministry. This applies to those who teach or preach.

16. It is not an assistant's job to bring _____ to the church.

> "An assistant's job is not to provide direction for the church, but to know the direction the pastor has established for the church, and to reinforce and assist in encouraging the people toward the fulfilling of that particular vision or direction."

17. Likewise, it is also not an assistant's job to provide _____ to the church body. By this, we mean an assistant should not have an agenda of trying to straighten out all the problems of the church when he or she is in the pulpit.

**Historical Marker**

"*He that is flexible shall not get bent out of shape.*"

–Unknown

**FUEL STOP**

**Proverbs 19:11**

11 The discretion of a man makes him slow to anger, And his glory is to overlook a transgression.

18. An assistant should not stir up problems that the pastor is going to have to clean up, or get into _____ subjects that are going to bring division and strife.

19. When teaching or preaching, an assistant should provide basic, _____ information that will reinforce the pulpit ministry that is taking place through the pastor.

20. **Trait #14:** Great supportive ministers demonstrate _____.

21. Discretion means that we have the wisdom to _____ and to _____ the right thing at the right time and at the right place.

22. What are some of the traits of people who have discretion?

   a) Their words and actions are in good taste.

   b) They carry themselves with a proper sense of _____ and respectability.

   c) They conduct themselves with an appropriate level of professionalism in their work and in their dealings with others.

   d) They respect the _____ of others and don't intrude inappropriately into another person's "private space."

e)  They demonstrate proper decorum, exhibiting politeness, courtesy, and good manners.

f)  They understand and follow the chain of command; they honor proper protocol in their conduct and communication.

g)  They show good _____ in handling difficult situations.

23. One of the primary areas of discretion is the ability to maintain _____.

24. Another trait of discretion is being able to keep your _____ under pressure. It also means that you carry yourself with _____, or with class.

## Historical Marker

*"All great players are self motivated."*
—Kevin McHale

# Inspection Station

1.  Which of the following is *not* a good reason to serve?

    a.  God has called us to do so.

    b.  We have an internal willingness to do so.

    c.  Someone makes us feel guilty or pressured from the outside.

    d.  We have an eagerness within that is birthed by the Holy Spirit.

    e.  We have a strong burning in our heart to please God and serve others.

2.  Examples of reports being provided in the Bible include:

    a.  The twelve spies reporting back after their trip into the Promised Land.

    b.  Jesus' disciples reporting back to Him after He had sent them out to minister.

### FUEL STOP

**1 Samuel 12:2–5 (NLT)**

2 Your king is now your leader. I stand here before you—an old, gray-haired man—and my sons serve you. I have served as your leader from the time I was a boy to this very day.

3 Now testify against me in the presence of the Lord and before his anointed one. Whose ox or donkey have I stolen? Have I ever cheated any of you? Have I ever oppressed you? Have I ever taken a bribe and perverted justice? Tell me and I will make right whatever I have done wrong."

4 "No," they replied, "you have never cheated or oppressed us, and you have never taken even a single bribe."

5 "The Lord and his anointed one are my witnesses today," Samuel declared, "that my hands are clean."

c. Paul and Barnabas reporting back to the Antioch church after their first missionary journey.

**Historical Marker**

*"It's not up to anyone else to make me give my best."*

–Hakeem Olajuwon

d. Paul received regular reports about the state of the churches from Timothy, Titus, and other associates.

e. All of the above

3. Which of the following is *not* an important part of delegation?

a. Being experienced in and knowledgeable enough about the position to know what it takes to be effective in that position

b. The ability to inspire others to become workers

c. Having a determination to continue doing all the work yourself

**FUEL STOP**

**1 Corinthians 9:22**

22 I have become all things to all men, that I might by all means save some.

d. Being willing to recruit others to become workers

e. Being able to train and supervise others, and at some point, releasing them to do the work

4. Samuel was an example of integrity because he:

a. Was called by God at a young age

b. Served the people without stealing, cheating, oppressing people, or taking bribes

c. Had visions and gave prophesies

d. Was a close, personal acquaintance of King Saul

e. All of the above

# Unpacking the Principles

1. What are the types of things that should change in a church, and what are the things that should never change? What is the difference between that which is negotiable and that which is nonnegotiable?

2. Review the traits of being a flexible, growth-oriented person on pages 108–109. Beside each of those statements, rate yourself on a scale of 1–10 (with 10 being excellent). In which aspects are you the strongest? Where can you improve?

3. In discussing taking initiative versus being amenable, what are some areas where a member or worker in the church can and should legitimately take initiative? What are examples of activities for which a member or worker should obtain permission through the proper channels before proceeding?

4. How are you doing in the area of communication? Are you keeping your supervisor properly apprised of important information regarding your area(s) of responsibility? Is there any way you might need to improve?

### Historical Marker

*"Nobody is going to wind you up every morning and give you a pep talk. So be a self starter."*

–Lou Holtz

5. In addition to being a good worker in the church, have you ever had the experience of inspiring others to become workers? Recruiting others? Training others? Supervising others? Can you think of anyone right now who you might be able to begin influencing in these ways?

6. Review the traits of being a person of honesty and integrity on page 110. Beside each of those statements, rate yourself on a scale of 1–10 (with 10 being excellent). In which aspects are you the strongest? Where can you improve?

7. Review the traits of being a person of discretion on pages 111–112. Beside each of those statements, rate yourself on a scale of 1–10 (with 10 being excellent). In which aspects are you the strongest? Where can you improve?

8. Review the scriptures in the Fuel Stops. Which one speaks the most to you about where you are in your walk with and service toward God? Why?

9. Review the quotes in the Historical Markers. Which one is the most meaningful to you? Why?

10. What is one thing you learned from this lesson that you can apply to your life? How can it enhance the way you serve?

### FUEL STOP

**2 Corinthians 8:3–5 (TLB)**

3 They gave not only what they could afford but far more; and I can testify that they did it because they wanted to and not because of nagging on my part.

4 They begged us to take the money so they could share in the joy of helping the Christians in Jerusalem.

5 Best of all, they went beyond our highest hopes, for their first action was to dedicate themselves to the Lord and to us, for whatever directions God might give to them through us.

**Off Road**

Jesse Owens is one of the great figures in track and field history. He went to the 1936 Olympics in Berlin and won four gold medals. Jesse said, "There is something that can happen to every athlete and every human being; the instinct to slack off, to give in to pain, to give less than your best; the instinct to hope you can win through luck or through your opponent not doing his best, instead of going to the limit and past your limit where victory is always found. Defeating those negative instincts that are out to defeat us is the difference between winning and losing—and we all face that battle every day."

 **Historical Marker**

"*Integrity is not a 90 percent thing, not a 95 percent thing; either you have it or you don't.*"

—Peter Scotese

Jesse used the term, "negative instincts," and said that we face a battle with them every day. What a need we have to stay at the top of our game. It reminds me of the admonition given in Hebrews 6:10–12: *"For God is not unjust to forget your work and labor of love which you have shown toward His name, in that you have ministered to the saints, and do minister. And we desire that each one of you show the same diligence to the full assurance of hope until the end, that you **do not become sluggish**, but imitate those who through faith and patience inherit the promises."*

 **FUEL STOP**

**2 Timothy 2:2**

2  And the things that you have heard from me among many witnesses, commit these to faithful men who will be able to teach others also.

How universal is this "negative instinct" to become sluggish? Very. A pastor friend of mine wrote the following memo to his leaders and asked me to review it before sending it.

Memo to: Church Leaders

God called me to start and pastor this church because He had need of it. We have an important, life-changing message that people need to hear. The Gospel is more than a message. It creates an atmosphere and produces an attitude. It involves a specific outlook toward God and His people, and ministers God's heart to them. Our faith influences the way we think, feel, and react to the daily situations and struggles we face.

Here is my concern: I need your help in caring for God's flock with all the conscientiousness of the True Shepherd. Not because you have to, but because you want to please God. Not viewing what we do as a job, but acting every day with eagerness. I need you to help me not just with presenting the message but also in demonstrating the atmosphere and attitude that is the word of faith at its best.

First Peter 5:2—4 (NLT) gives me as the senior pastor instructions as to how I am to do my job: *"Care for the flock that God has entrusted to you. Watch over it willingly, not grudgingly—not for what you will get out of it, but because you are eager to serve God. Don't lord it over the people assigned to your care, but lead them by your own good example. And when the Great Shepherd appears, you will receive a crown of never-ending glory and honor."*

I need you to be here for the same reasons for which I am here and for the same purpose that God has in His mind. We are to bless people and be their servants.

I see that we have let some things slip concerning the atmosphere we are creating and presenting. So I want us to "kick it up a notch" concerning our enthusiasm level and our watchfulness to represent the right teaching, atmosphere, and attitude to everyone. If things are troubling you, we need to deal with them. If people are troubling you, we have a grievance procedure in the church to follow. Let's use it. We must convey a loving, encouraging excitement about what God is doing here and not be passive, critical, or condemning. We must look for the positives and minimize and eliminate the negatives, not only from our own souls but also, hopefully, from the souls of those we work with as well.

Together we are building the kingdom of God. I appreciate each of you for your help and the unique strength you add to the overall expression of our local church. From one who watches for your souls, grace and peace be with you.

*Pastor Jim*

When I read that letter, I thought it was an excellent communiqué: encouraging, challenging, and uplifting. Ultimately, though, the pastor elected not to send it. He was concerned that it might come across as negative or condemning. I certainly respected his decision, but it made me wonder how many pastors across the country would like to say the same types of things to their key leaders but haven't. Let's let the above words be a challenge to us all and not grow sluggish or allow "negative instincts" to overcome us.

# Travelogue

# Travelogue

# Lesson 13

## Packing for the Trip

🚗 In the textbook, *In Search of Timothy*, read

- The introduction to Part IV, "Staying Free From Staff Infection"

- Chapter 29, "Avoiding Staff Infection"

- Chapter 30, "Under the Influence" through the section called "Yielding to the Devil's Influence"

🚗 Watch Lesson 13 on DVD

🚗 Work through this chapter in the workbook

 ## The Expressway

If the immune system of the human body breaks down or is weakened, the body is more vulnerable to infection. Likewise, there are conditions in the Body of Christ—in terms of our relationship with each other—that can make us more prone to experiencing "infection." In other words, we can have unnecessary tension, turmoil, and strife in our relationships.

People often start serving God with zeal and idealism, but often drift into apathy or become distracted by personality conflicts, bad attitudes, or wrong spiritual influences. Most people in the church are supportive and good-hearted, but others can be non-supportive critics and complainers.

Three factors that can lower our spiritual immune system and make us more vulnerable to staff infection are fatigue, flattery, and frustrations. Frustrations are often due to unrealistic expectations.

Every church has problems because every church has people. If we are wise and mature, we will focus on the purpose of the church and work at being a part of the solution. Anyone can sit back and criticize the imperfections.

Staff infection is found all through the Bible. For example, Adam blamed Eve, Cain killed Abel, and so forth. Jesus even had to deal with staff infection among His disciples. Relationships have always provided opportunities for strife and turmoil, but our challenge is to rise above those and stay on track with God's purpose.

 **Historical Marker**

> *"Every small group has at least one 'difficult' person in it. If you don't immediately recognize who that person is—it's probably you."*
>
> –Rick Warren

 # The Scenic Route

1.  It is possible to maintain healthy relationships in working for God, but many times, even in church relationships, people get in _____ with one another. People develop _____ problems.

2.  If we don't keep the right attitude, we can lose our _____ in serving God, and instead of being thankful for the privilege of serving God, we begin to see it as drudgery, a _____ and an obligation. God has not called us to go into spiritual retirement, but we are supposed to serve Him with gladness and joy until we go to _____.

 **FUEL STOP**

**Luke 22:24–27**

24 Now there was also a dispute among them, as to which of them should be considered the greatest.

25 And He said to them, "The kings of the Gentiles exercise lordship over them, and those who exercise authority over them are called 'benefactors.'

26 But not so among you; on the contrary, he who is greatest among you, let him be as the younger, and he who governs as he who serves.

27 For who is greater, he who sits at the table, or he who serves? Is it not he who sits at the table? Yet I am among you as the One who serves."

3. Infection most often comes into the body of Christ through _____ problems—strife, personality differences, difficulties when people perhaps even yield to a wrong spiritual influence.

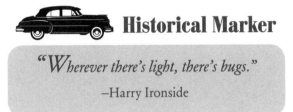

## Historical Marker

*"Wherever there's light, there's bugs."*
—Harry Ironside

"While things may happen in the natural that tend to irritate us, it is important to know that the fruit of the spirit is a more powerful force, and should be a more predominant factor in our life, than little fleshly irritations that we might experience. We're commanded to walk in the love of God."

4. When we recognize how many problems leaders face, it should cause us to have the attitude of: "Lord, help me to be a _____ to my pastor. Help me to be an encouragement to him, and to be an asset and not a _____."

5. As it is with our human body physically, there are factors that can lower our immune system _____ and make us more susceptible to infection. There are factors that can make us more vulnerable to the kind of strife, tension, and friction that can be destructive and make church relationships _____.

### FUEL STOP

**Galatians 6:9–10**

9 And let us not grow weary while doing good, for in due season we shall reap if we do not lose heart.

10 Therefore, as we have opportunity, let us do good to all, especially to those who are of the household of faith.

## Three Factors that Can Lower our Spiritual Immune System:

6. **Factor #1:** _____

7. There are several adjectives that describe what happens when people become fatigued, weary, worn out, and exhausted. List some of them. They become more _____ _____ _____ .

8. People often have not established the discipline and priority of 1) seeking _____ the Kingdom of God; and 2) developing a principle of _____ in their lives.

"We are not under the Old Testament law of the Sabbath, but there is a Sabbath principle that God established that is very relevant to and important for our lives today."

9. God may lead some people to _____ their lives—to say _____ to some things so they can say _____ to the most important things.

10. **Factor #2:** _____

11. Flattery is an issue that is connected directly to the _____.

12. When people succumb to the influence of flattery, it ceases to be a _____ effort where we're all working together to bless the body of Christ. It then becomes a _____ where one person is trying to outdo somebody else and is trying to prove that he or she is better.

13. **Factor #3:** _____

14. Practically speaking, there is no such thing as a _____ church. Every church has _____.

**FUEL STOP**

**John 21:19–22**

19 . . . He [Jesus] said to him [Peter], "Follow Me."

20 Then Peter, turning around, saw the disciple whom Jesus loved following, who also had leaned on His breast at the supper, and said, "Lord, who is the one who betrays You?"

21 Peter, seeing him, said to Jesus, "But Lord, what about this man?"

22 Jesus said to him, "If I will that he remain till I come, what is that to you? You follow Me."

"One of the greatest weapons that Satan uses against churches is to get individuals into a spirit of criticism and faultfinding—where their focus is on what's wrong with the church. People sit back and become judges and analysts. They're not necessarily doing anything to contribute to the improvement of the church; they're simply sitting back, judging, analyzing, and critiquing. That does nothing though to build up the church."

15. One of the reasons why people so easily fall prey to frustration has to do with the kinds of _____ they have. Without even realizing it, we can become a perfectionist in our expectations. We judge everything against an _____ that doesn't really exist. The difference between the ideal and the real becomes the measure of _____, or the measure of frustration.

16. Staff infection happened throughout the _____.

17. One moment, Peter said to Jesus, *"You are the Christ . . ."* (Matt. 16:16), whereupon Jesus said Peter's words were inspired by God. Shortly after that, when Jesus said he had to go to Jerusalem and die, Peter took Jesus aside and began to _____ Him. What do we learn from this? People can be used by the Spirit of _____ one moment and then yield to a _____ spiritual influence the next.

## Historical Marker

*"Be realistic.*
*Lower your expectations of earth.*
*This is not heaven, so don't expect it to be."*

–Max Lucado

## Inspection Station

1.  In the teaching, EGR stood for:

    a.  Every Good Report

    b.  Extra Grace Required

    c.  Extravagant Giving Requested

    d.  Eventual Good Results

    e.  Expecting Great Recruits

**FUEL STOP**

**1 Corinthians 12:27**
27 Now you are the body of Christ, and members individually.

2.  Which of the following is an example of a non-supportive, problematic type of person in a church?

    a.  Opinionated critics and complainers

    b.  One who wants, expects, and demands that everything be done his way

    c.  A wet blanket–someone who is negative and pessimistic

    d.  One who gossips and spreads discontent

    e.  All of the above

3. Which of the following is *not* an example of staff infection that was reported in the Bible?

    a. Cain killing Abel

    b. Adam blaming Eve

    c. Jesus washing the feet of the disciples

    d. Competition between Peter and John

    e. The Corinthians getting drunk at communion services

## Historical Marker

*"Fatigue makes cowards of us all."*

–Coach Vince Lombardi

# Unpacking the Principles

1. How are you doing in terms of keeping your joy, peace, and zeal in serving God? Are you at high levels in those areas, or do you need to regain some lost ground? If so, what do you need to do to return to your earlier, higher levels?

2. Based on the admonitions in the first few verses of Ephesians chapter 4, how are you doing in the area of forbearing others in love? Of being humble, gentle, and patient? Of making allowances for each other's faults? Of endeavoring to keep the unity of the Spirit in the bond of peace?

3. How are you doing in terms of keeping yourself from fatigue? Are you living a life that is properly paced so you have enough time and energy to serve God effectively? Are your priorities in good order, enabling you to seek first the Kingdom of God? Are you observing the *principle* of Sabbath in your life?

4. Have you ever allowed flattery to influence you inappropriately? Have you ever treated ministry as though it was a popularity contest, or allowed yourself to get into competition with someone else in the church? If so, what did you do to correct yourself?

5. How are you doing in the area of frustration? Are you keeping your expectations reasonable? Are you appropriately striving for improvement without allowing yourself to become excessively frustrated with problems?

## FUEL STOP

**Ephesians 4:1–3 (NLT)**

1 Therefore I, a prisoner for serving the Lord, beg you to lead a life worthy of your calling, for you have been called by God.

2 Always be humble and gentle. Be patient with each other, making allowance for each other's faults because of your love.

3 Make every effort to keep yourselves united in the Spirit, binding yourselves together with peace.

## FUEL STOP

**Ephesians 4:1–3**

1 I, therefore, the prisoner of the Lord, beseech you to walk worthy of the calling with which you were called,

2 with all lowliness and gentleness, with longsuffering, bearing with one another in love,

3 endeavoring to keep the unity of the Spirit in the bond of peace.

6. Review the scriptures in the Fuel Stops. Which one speaks the most to you about where you are in your walk with and service toward God? Why?

7. Review the quotes in the Historical Markers. Which one is the most meaningful to you? Why?

8. What is one thing you learned from this lesson that you can apply to your life? How can it enhance the way you serve?

 **Off Road**

Teddy Roosevelt expressed great wisdom and insight when he said: "It's not the critic who counts: not the man who points out how the strong man stumbles or when the doer of deeds could have done better. The credit belongs to the man who is actually in the arena, whose face is marred by dust and sweat and blood, who strives valiantly, who errs and comes short again and again, because there is no effort without error or shortcoming, but who knows the great enthusiasms, the great devotions, who spends himself in a worthy cause; who, at the best, knows, in the end, the triumph of high achievement, and who, at the worst, if he fails, at least fails while daring greatly, so that his place shall never be with those cold and timid souls who know neither victory or defeat."

Roosevelt understood the difference between the doer and the critic, and we would all do well to ask ourselves into which category we fit? Even if we do it imperfectly, we need to be that person "in the arena."

Another great leader, Abraham Lincoln, also resolved himself to be one of those individuals committed to action. He also had to rise above the voices of the critics in his accomplishments. He said, "If I tried to read, much less answer, all the criticisms made of me, this office would have to be closed for all other business. I do the best I know how, the very best I can. And I mean to keep on doing this, down to the very end. If the end brings me out

 **Historical Marker**

*"It is easy to become discouraged by the gap between the ideal and the real in your church. Yet we must passionately love the church in spite of its imperfections. Longing for the ideal while criticizing the real is evidence of immaturity. On the other hand, settling for the real without striving for the ideal is complacency. Maturity is living with the tension."*

—Rick Warren

all wrong, ten angels swearing I had been right would make no difference. If the end brings me out all right, then what is said against me now will not amount to anything."

We can draw from this two great lessons and decisions:

1. We will be doers, achievers, and accomplishers.

2. We will not sit passively by and criticize those who are doing the work.

 **Historical Marker**

"*Farewell to those who want an entirely pure and purified church. This is plainly wanting no church at all.*"

—Martin Luther

## Travelogue

_____

_____

_____

_____

_____

_____

_____

_____

_____

_____

# Travelogue

# Travelogue

# Lesson 14

## Packing for the Trip

- In the textbook, *In Search of Timothy*, read

  - Chapter 30, "Under the Influence" beginning with the section titled, "James and John: The Sons of Thunder"

  - Chapter 31, "Know Who You Work For"

  - Chapter 32, "Offense Can Kill You"

  - Chapter 33, "Absalom: The Ultimate Staff Infection"

- Watch Lesson 14 on DVD

- Work through this chapter in the workbook

## The Expressway

In this series, we've been searching for Timothy, i.e., identifying the traits of those who function in the same way Timothy did toward Paul. Their hearts are committed to serve, help, and assist. They are committed to stand alongside their pastor and give of their time, talents, and abilities to help further the purpose of God.

## Historical Marker

*"It's no compliment to be a called
a problem spotter,
but the world loves problem solvers."*

—Mark Sanborn

Continuing the discussion on staff infection, we see how Jesus dealt with staff infection among His disciples. Under Moses' leadership, the people became impatient during Moses' absence and pressured Aaron to do something contrary to God's plan—to erect a golden calf as an idol. Wanting to be popular more than wanting to lead by principle, Aaron yielded to the pressure of the people. This brought great staff infection among God's people, and Moses had to deal with it. Ahithophel never forgave David for his transgression against Bathsheba, and the resentment and offense in his heart brought him into union with another victim, and carrier, of staff infection, Absalom.

The Bible is full of stories about staff infection, and we need to be on guard against any kind of attitude problem, rebellion, and attitudes of criticism or faultfinding that would make us a part of something other than the unity that God desires for the body of Christ. We need each other, and we must recognize not only the gifts we have, but also the gifts we don't have. That means we need to lean on each other and respect each other's gifts. When we do that, we then can operate in the divine connections and partnerships that God intends, and His Spirit can work with us in that kind of unity.

### FUEL STOP

**Luke 9:54–56**

54 And when His disciples James and John saw this, they said, "Lord, do You want us to command fire to come down from heaven and consume them, just as Elijah did?"

55 But He turned and rebuked them, and said, "You do not know what manner of spirit you are of.

56 For the Son of Man did not come to destroy men's lives but to save them." And they went to another village.

## The Scenic Route

"A Timothy is someone whose heart is committed to serve, help, and assist. Timothys are committed to stand alongside of and serve with a pastor or a spiritual leader and give their gifts, time, ability, and talent to help the vision and purpose that originates in the heart of God come to pass. This is not about exalting a leader—putting a leader on a pedestal for the sake of worship—but it acknowledges the fact that when God does things in the earth, He raises up leaders. He puts mission, vision, assignments, and dreams in those leaders' hearts. Yet those leaders can never fulfill that without the assistance and help—not only of God spiritually, but also of anointed, called people in the ministry of helps, or supportive ministry."

1. When James and John wanted to call fire down on the Samaritan village, Jesus _____ them and told them that He had not come to destroy men's lives, but to _____ them.

2. Part of Jesus' rebuke involved telling James and John that they didn't know the type of spirit they were being _____ by.

3. We can't have an attitude of strife and division in the body of Christ if we are going to be _____ as believers.

4. At times, Aaron was a _____ to Moses, and at times, he was a _____.

5. Aaron's job, when Moses was on the mountain, was to represent _____ to the people. Instead, he yielded to _____ from the people. Aaron may have done that because he wanted to be _____ and wanted everyone to like him.

6. Ahithophel was an _____ to King David and to Absalom. When he gave advice, it was just like _____ talking.

7. The question that comes to mind when considering Ahithophel pertains to how he could have been so wise but so _____.

8. Ahithophel stands as a monumental lesson that we cannot afford to harbor offense, resentment, grudges, or unforgiveness about _____.

9. It's interesting that Ahithophel and Absalom joined forces. Ahithophel was offended at what David _____. Absalom was offended at what David did _____ do. In both cases, there was offense, and in both cases, the individuals suffered greatly because of it.

⛽ **FUEL STOP**

**Matthew 5:9**
9 Blessed are the peacemakers, For they shall be called sons of God.

10. We need to be on _____ against any kind of attitude problem, rebellion, and attitudes of criticism and faultfinding that would make us a part of something other than the unity that God desires for the body of Christ.

11. Every single one of us is _____ by design. We're all lacking something. If we are going to function well, we've got to:

   a) Be _____ about what we're lacking and realize that we don't have every gift there is to have.

   b) Lean on other people.

   c) Be willing to use the gifts we have in _____ with others and the gifts they have.

 **Inspection Station**

1. James and John had the nickname of Boanerges, which means:

   a. Sons of Comfort

   b. Sons of Consolation

   c. Sons of Thunder

   d. Sons of Authority

   e. Sons of Encouragement

 **FUEL STOP**

**Proverbs 14:30**

30 A sound heart is life to the body, But envy is rottenness to the bones.

2. Which apostle wrote about the wisdom that is from above—which is pure, peaceful, and gentle—and the wisdom that is earthly, sensual, and demonic?

   a. Paul

   b. James

   c. John

   d. Jude

   e. Peter

3.  Which of the following statements is true of Ahithophel?

    a.  He was very wise but not loyal.

    b.  He harbored great offense in his heart against David.

    c.  He apparently never forgave David for his sin against Bathsheba.

    d.  When his advice was not followed, Ahithophel took his own life.

    e.  All of the above

**FUEL STOP**

**Proverbs 21:2**
2 Every way of a man is right in his own eyes, But the Lord weighs the hearts.

4.  Which of the following statements is true of Absalom?

    a.  Absalom was offended because King David took no action regarding the rape of his sister, Tamar.

    b.  Absalom was a self-promoter; he drew people unto himself.

    c.  Absalom attempted to discredit and undermine the leadership of David.

    d.  Absalom stole the hearts of the people.

    e.  All of the above

 **Historical Marker**

"*It's more important to get along with people than to get ahead of them.*"

–John Maxwell

# Unpacking the Principles

1.  Having studied the traits and characteristics of Timothy throughout this series, in what ways do you feel you're demonstrating those traits? What are your areas of strength, and in what ways do you need to grow the most?

2.  James and John had trouble with reacting to others angrily. How do you do in this regard? Do you keep your cool and walk in love even when others are wrong? Do you tend to react in anger? What do you need to do to make sure that your actions remain godly and Christlike?

3.  It appears that Aaron gave in to the pressure of the people because he wanted to be popular. He violated "principle" in order to pursue popularity. Have you ever felt that type of pressure? What did you do about it?

4. Ahithophel had a major problem when his advice was not followed and when things weren't done the way he thought they should be done. How are you in this regard? Do you get offended when things aren't done the way you think they should be?

5. Overall, do you think you're doing a good job of staying free from "Staff Infection?" Are you contributing to peace and unity within the church family?

6. What does being "deficient by design" mean to you? Are you comfortable with the gifts and abilities you don't have, as well as with the ones you do possess? Do you believe you're properly connected with others who have and are using gifts you don't have?

 **Historical Marker**

> *"The key to everything is patience. You get the chicken by hatching the egg, not smashing it."*
>
> –Arnold Glasow

7. Review the scriptures in the Fuel Stops. Which one speaks the most to you about where you are in your walk with and service toward God? Why?

8. Review the quotes in the Historical Markers. Which one is the most meaningful to you? Why?

9. What is one thing you learned from this lesson that you can apply to your life? How can it enhance the way you serve?

 **Off Road**

Revelation chapters 2 and 3 are unique in Scripture, because they contain the words of Jesus speaking to local churches. Jesus spoke words of commendation and correction to these churches. Only the congregations of Smyrna and Philadelphia received no correction, and the church at Laodicea received no commendation. There were three thoughts, though, that were communicated consistently to all seven churches. Because of the repetition, I can only assume that these three issues were extremely important to Jesus in the operation and health of every local church, both then and now. To each of the seven churches Jesus said:

- "I know your works."

- "He that has an ear, let him hear what the Spirit is saying to the churches."

- "He that overcomes . . ."

 **FUEL STOP**

**Acts 20:28–30**

28 Therefore take heed to yourselves and to all the flock, among which the Holy Spirit has made you overseers, to shepherd the church of God which He purchased with His own blood.

29 For I know this, that after my departure savage wolves will come in among you, not sparing the flock.

30 Also from among yourselves men will rise up, speaking perverse things, to draw away the disciples after themselves.

## Historical Marker

> *"If you are not a peacemaker, at least do not be a troublemaker."*
>
> –Saint Isaac the Syrian

It seems logical that Jesus wants every church to be a working church, a listening church, and an overcoming church. Much could be said about each of these issues, but let's look for a moment at the issue of being a working church.

Titus has been called "The Book of Good Works." In this epistle written to a young pastor, Paul reminded Titus that God's grace alone is the source of our salvation. *"But when the kindness and the love of God our Savior toward man appeared, NOT BY WORKS OF RIGHTEOUSNESS WHICH WE HAVE DONE, BUT ACCORDING TO HIS MERCY HE SAVED US, through the washing of regeneration and renewing of the Holy Spirit, whom He poured out on us abundantly through Jesus Christ our Savior, that HAVING BEEN JUSTIFIED BY HIS GRACE we should become heirs according to the hope of eternal life"* (Titus 3:4–7).

This same book, which makes it so plain that works are not the *cause* of our salvation also makes it abundantly clear that works–good works–are a most appropriate *result* of our salvation:

- Titus 2:7–*"in all things showing yourself to be A PATTERN OF GOOD WORKS. . . ."*

- Titus 2:14–*"who gave Himself for us, that He might redeem us from every lawless deed and purify for Himself His own special people, ZEALOUS FOR GOOD WORKS."*

- Titus 3:8–*". . . those who have believed in God should BE CAREFUL TO MAINTAIN GOOD WORKS. These things are good and profitable to men."*

- Titus 3:14–*"And let our people also LEARN TO MAINTAIN GOOD WORKS, to meet urgent needs, that they may not be unfruitful."*

One of the reasons why churches need to stay free from strife and division is so they can stay focused on the work that Jesus wants us to accomplish. Infighting and controversy always seem to take our eyes off of our purpose and sidetrack us from the work He wants us to do.

Remember, Jesus wants every church to be a working church, a listening church, and an overcoming church!

 **FUEL STOP**

**Mark 10:35–37, 41–45**

35 Then James and John, the sons of Zebedee, came to Him, saying, "Teacher, we want You to do for us whatever we ask."

36 And He said to them, "What do you want Me to do for you?"

37 They said to Him, "Grant us that we may sit, one on Your right hand and the other on Your left, in Your glory."

41 And when the ten heard it, they began to be greatly displeased with James and John.

42 But Jesus called them to Himself and said to them, "You know that those who are considered rulers over the Gentiles lord it over them, and their great ones exercise authority over them.

43 Yet it shall not be so among you; but whoever desires to become great among you shall be your servant.

44 And whoever of you desires to be first shall be slave of all.

45 For even the Son of Man did not come to be served, but to serve, and to give His life a ransom for many."

# Travelogue

# Lesson 1

## The Scenic Route

1. leaders
2. committed
3. God, pastor, each other
4. unity
5. **Supportive:** Something that supports, provides stability, or lends strength. It undergirds and assists.
   **Minister:** Someone who serves.
6. God has called each of us to assist, to provide stability, to lend strength, to undergird, and to offer support through serving. We're all called to be supportive ministers.
7. title
8. example
9. We learn that if people will function as "one" and speak the same language, nothing they imagine will be impossible to them.
10. First: leader. Examples: Moses, Deborah, David, Elijah, Nehemiah, Paul, and so forth.
    Second: vision. Definition: A vision simply means they have a mental or a spiritual picture of the way things could be, or the way things should be as a desired future.
    Third: I, people
11. alone, helps
12. failure, success, minimized

## Inspection Station

1. b. Discouraged by how poorly church leadership teams functioned in terms of harmony and unity
2. d. Equip believers so that everyone can be involved in getting the work done
3. c. Those who were the most faithful to serve
4. b. Moses (Exod. 4:10)
5. c. Gideon (Judges 6:15)
6. d. Jeremiah (Jer. 1:6)

# Lesson 2

## The Scenic Route

1c. assistants
1e. 30%
2a. relative
3. God the Father
4. Jesus
5. angels
6. Lucifer
7. Adam, Eve
8. the 12 disciples
9. Peter (John 18:10)
10. Judas Iscariot (John 12:6)
11. perfect
12. follower-ship

## Inspection Station

1. e. All of the above
2. c. Paul was full of self-pity and felt sorry for himself.
3. d. All of the above

# Lesson 3

## The Scenic Route

1. Jethro, delegation
2. small or basic, great or difficult
3. easier, endure
4. afflicted, burden
5. die
6. We can assist our pastor.
7. recipients, conduits
8. use, using
9. want, need
10. important

## Inspection Station

1. c. Advice from his father-in-law
2. e. All of the above
3. e. All of the above

## Lesson 4

### The Scenic Route

1. important, small
2. pastor
3. outside, inside
4. Jesus
5. accident, develop
6. God, Word
7. relationship
8. substitute
9. productivity, transformation
10. church
11. calling, preach, scenes
12. pastor
13. recognition

### Inspection Station

1. e. All of the above
2. d. The church at Ephesus
3. a. They might be with Him.
4. e. All of the above
5. b. It is vital that our calling be dramatic and sensational. Those who are called through a dream, an audible voice, or an angelic appearance will always have the most effective ministries.

## Lesson 5

### The Scenic Route

1. leader, vision
2. participants, spectators
3. calling, supportive, scenes
4a. purpose
4b. office
4c. personality
5. come, change
6. familiarity
7. anointed
8. fearful
9. agenda

### Characteristics of a Timothy

1. trust
2. encourage, troubled
3. accountable
4. like-, soul, priorities
5. cares, hireling
6. self-

### Inspection Station

1. e. All of the above
2. c. Because of the sanctification and spirituality of all believers, it is likely that we will never be "rubbed the wrong way" by anyone else's personality or see anything in other believers or leaders that would disappoint us.
3. a. They were astonished at Jesus' wisdom and works.
4. e. All of the above

## Lesson 6

### The Scenic Route

1. position, heart
2. proven
3. with
4. gifts
5. interdependent
6. respectful, critical
7. profitable or useful
8. failed
9. attitude, developed
10. team, partnership
11. followers, leaders
12. friends
13. relational
14. working
14d. organizational
14e. finances

**Inspection Station**
1. e. All of the above
2. b. Paul wanted to give Mark a second chance, but Barnabas refused.
3. c. By the coming of Titus
4. b. Onesiphorus
5. e. Ordinary

# Lesson 7

**The Scenic Route**
1. ordinary
2. assignment
3. mistakes
3a. fire
3c. feed
3d. children
4. misrepresented
5. with
6. everyone
6a. prayer
6b. arms
6c. lead, fight
7. done, success
8. himself
9a. Stand
9b. work
9c. select
9d. let
10. pastor, equip
11. die
12. titles, Spirit
13. minded
14. blueprint

**Inspection Station**
1. c. Referring to Jesus, John the Baptist said, "He must decrease, but I must increase."
2. e. All of the above
3. b. When God placed the same Spirit on Moses' leaders, it made all of them (including Moses) coequal in leadership.

# Lesson 8

**The Scenic Route**
1. decides
2. covenant
3. convenient
4. support, John, Baptist
5. Jonathan
6. worship, purpose
7a. peace
7b. help
7c. united
8. congregation, core
9. expected
10a. Paul
10b. Spirit
10c. David
11. yours, help
12. broke, offering, worship
13. Elisha, water, served

**Inspection Station**
1. c. The soul of Jonathan was knit to the soul of David.
2. b. Jonathan's armor bearer to Jonathan
3. b. Communicating expectations about the motives and attitudes he expected if they were to unite with him
4. e. All of the above

# Lesson 9

**The Scenic Route**
1. traits
2. loyalty
3. rebellion
4. Ruth
5. David
6. Joab
7. extension, representative
8. attitude
9. ability, gifts
10. problems, low, high

11. frustrated, good
12. faithful
13. small
14. availability
15a. reliable
15e. starter
15g. Punctual
15j. Honest
16. count, trust
17. Joseph

**Inspection Station**

1. e. All of the above
2. c. It's okay if people compliment us while criticizing the senior pastor.
3. a. Our attitude is just one of many situations in life that we have no control over.
4. e. All of the above

# Lesson 10

**The Scenic Route**

1. faithfulness
2. served
3. attitude
4. best, best
5. mental
6. blessing
7. helps
8. self-
9. function
10a. authority
10c. oversee
11. submission
12. joy, grief
13d. stubborn
14. joy
14e. serve

**Inspection Station**

1. c. They believed they needed to keep their focus on prayer and the ministry of the Word.
2. d. Be willing to serve
3. e. All of the above

# Lesson 11

**The Scenic Route**

1. strife
2. teamwork
3. competition
4. completing
5. supervision, diplomacy
6. servant's
7. personified
8. enthusiastic
9. motivated
10. dead
11. balanced
12. rest
13a. worship
13c. rest
14. tasks
15. earthly, supernatural
16. humor

**Inspection Station**

1. b. Jesus did not come to serve, but to be served.
2. e. All of the above
3. c. Nehemiah
4. a. Epaphroditus

# Lesson 12

**The Scenic Route**

1. flexible
2. dying
3a. learners
3c. ideas
3g. improvement
4. inside
5. make
6. answer, permission
7. listener
8. reports
9. multiply

10. develop
11. recruiting
12. integrity
13a. pure
13c. truth
13e. impression
13g. promises
14. trust
15. pulpit
16. direction
17. correction
18. controversial
19. helpful
20. discretion
21. say, do
22b. dignity
22d. boundaries
22g. judgment
23. confidentiality
24. cool, dignity

**Inspection Station**

1. c. Someone makes us feel guilty or pressured from the outside.
2. e. All of the above
3. c. Having a determination to continue doing all the work yourself
4. b. Served the people without stealing, cheating, oppressing people, or taking bribes

# Lesson 13

**The Scenic Route**

1. strife, attitude
2. joy, chore, heaven
3. relationship
4. blessing, liability
5. spiritually, unpleasant
6. fatigue
7. irritable, grouchy, cranky, grumpy, edgy, and so forth
8. first, Sabbath

9. simplify, no, yes
10. flattery
11. ego
12. team, competition
13. frustration
14. perfect, problems
15. expectations, ideal, disappointment
16. Bible
17. rebuke, God, wrong

**Inspection Station**

1. b. Extra Grace Required
2. e. All of the above
3. c. Jesus washing the feet of the disciples

# Lesson 14

**The Scenic Route**

1. rebuked, save
2. influenced
3. healthy
4. blessing, detriment
5. Moses, pressure, popular
6. advisor, God
7. disloyal
8. anything
9. did, not
10. guard
11. deficient
11a. honest
11c. partnership

**Inspection Station**

1. c. Sons of Thunder
2. b. James
3. e. All of the above
4. e. All of the above

# Endnotes

**Lesson 2**

[1] Taken from *A Tale of Three Kings* by Gene Edwards. Copyright © 1980 and 1992 by Gene Edwards. Used by permission of Tyndale House Publishers, Inc. All rights reserved.

**Lesson 6**

[1] Lawrence J. Crabb, Jr., *Encouragement: The Key to Caring* (Grand Rapids: Zondervan Publishing House, 1984), 24–25.

**Lesson 7**

[1] Roger J. Dow, *Turned On: Eight Vital Insights to Energize Your People, Customers, and Profits* (New York: HarperCollins Publishers, Inc.,1997), 42. Used by permission.

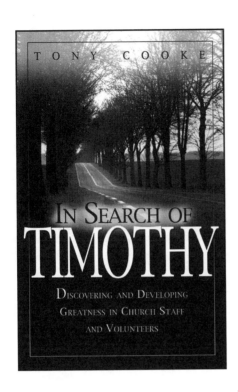

## IN SEARCH OF TIMOTHY

### TONY COOKE

Good leadership works to its optimum potential with good followers. Leaders must be supported by men and women who will respond to God's call for excellence in supportive ministry.

ISBN-10: 0-89276-973-4 / ISBN-13: 978-0-89276-973-5

## IN SEARCH OF TIMOTHY COMPLETE LEADERSHIP TRAINING COURSE

### TONY COOKE

Pastors and leaders everywhere are looking for those who will help them fulfill their God-given mandate. Young Timothy serves as a sterling example for Christians to follow and emulate. In this curriculum, Tony Cooke explores the spiritual and practical steps that are necessary to becoming a Timothy. It's time to gear up, because you were created by God to make a significant impact in your church!

*Curriculum Includes:*

- 14 Video Lessons on 5 DVDs
- 14 Audio Lessons on 7 CDs
- Paperback Book
- Workbook
- Leader's Guide
- Advertising Poster

ISBN-10: 0-89276-982-3 / ISBN-13: 978-0-89276-982-7

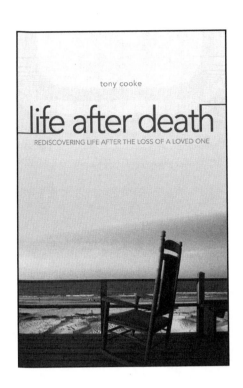

# LIFE AFTER DEATH

*Rediscovering Life After the Loss of a Loved One*

## TONY COOKE

Are you grieving? Do you know someone who is? Rev. Cooke's book contains insights from God's Word and personal reflections from those who have walked the road you or someone you know may now be walking.

ISBN-10: 0-89276-966-1 / ISBN-13: 978-0-89276-966-7

If you would like to contact the author,

you may do so through

**www.tonycooke.org**.

Tony Cooke

www.tonycooke.org